THE LAST LINE OF DEFENSE

THE LAST LINE
OF DEFENSE

The New Fight for American Liberty

Ken Cuccinelli

with Brian J. Gottstein

CROWN
FORUM
NEW YORK

Library of Congress Cataloging-in-Publication Data
is available upon request.

ISBN 978-0-770-43709-1
eISBN 978-0-770-43710-7

Printed in the United States of America

Jacket design by Michael Nagin

2 4 6 8 10 9 7 5 3 1

First Edition

When a president is willing to repeatedly disregard the law to

force his radical policies on the American people,

we become the last line of defense against

a government out of control.

CONTENTS

FOREWORD

by Senator Jim DeMint

M ORE THAN TWO centuries ago, thirteen American states, after winning their hard-fought independence from the most powerful military in the world, joined together to assure that future generations of Americans would never again be subservient to a central power. Representatives from every state signed a contract to form a federal government that would provide for their mutual defense, facilitate interstate commerce, and guarantee liberty for all citizens.

This contract—the Constitution of the United States—specifically limited the powers of the federal government to a short list of enumerated functions, and the accompanying Bill of Rights stated explicitly that all other policy matters would be left to the people and the states. The Constitution is not a piece of legislation that can be changed merely by a vote in Congress or waived by a presidential edict. It is a legally binding contract between two parties—the American people and their federal government—that must be protected by the states and enforced by our courts.

However, state and federal judges have for too long looked the other way as politicians and unelected bureaucrats have systematically violated this contract and eroded the liberties of the American people in the process. For decades, congressmen, senators, and presidents of both parties have run roughshod over constitutional limits and created unsustainable levels of debt and dysfunction.

I can say with some authority after fourteen years in the U.S. House and Senate that too many federal politicians—no matter which party is in power—will continue to spend, borrow, and grow the federal government until it eventually collapses under its own weight.

They will continue to try to fix problems caused by excessive government with more government programs and spending, all while extracting more and more money and liberty from the people. Unless the states demand that the courts enforce the contractual limits of federal power, the federal government will fail, and it will bring the states and the people down with it.

Ken Cuccinelli's *The Last Line of Defense* provides freedom-loving Americans and our states with the blueprint to save America and the cause of liberty. Ken has a brilliant legal mind and is a rare package of intellect, courage, and tenacity . . . all with a winsome presentation of the benefits of liberty and limited government. As attorney general of Virginia, he has boldly demonstrated how states can begin to restrain the ever-growing federal behemoth.

For example, Ken, in tandem with twenty-seven other state attorneys general, brought a lawsuit against the government to stop the federal takeover of America's health care system. The states won the central constitutional argument of the case, and except for some inexplicable tortured logic by the chief justice of the Supreme Court, Americans would have been saved from another imposition on their liberty and another debt-ridden federal program. While the overall case was lost, that effort has inspired states to work together to attempt to force the federal government to live within the restraints of the Constitution.

In several other instances, such as with the EPA and the National Labor Relations Board, the states have been and continue to be successful in pushing back against the federal government. This book explains how they are doing it.

States are leading in other ways as well. While the bad news is that the federal government appears to be headed toward a meltdown, the good news is that many states are demonstrating how responsible, limited government can work for the benefit of every citizen. For example, many states have passed right-to-work laws that protect the rights of workers not to join a union. The result has been a more attractive environment for business, more jobs, and increased tax revenues without raising taxes. Those states are also improving education with more school choice; creating business-friendly environments with fewer regulations, fewer taxes, and better protection from predatory lawsuits; and improving family life by upholding traditional values.

Unfortunately, there are other states run by liberal-progressive politicians that foolishly continue to move in the opposite direction: raising taxes, increasing regulations, expanding unionization, growing government and debt, and replacing voluntary societal values with provably destructive politically correct government values.

Because of these policies, many of these liberal-progressive states will be bankrupt within the next five to ten years as a result of bloated budgets, unfunded pension plans, and antibusiness policies. Some of these governments are already looking to the federal government for your tax dollars to bail them out from their own irresponsible decisions. These states will also try to use the federal government to stop the advance of liberty in other states. They will attempt to pass federal legislation or secure court rulings to stop school choice and will try to use federal policies to impose on other states the same onerous taxes, expensive regulations, and high-energy costs that have chased their own citizens, businesses, and prosperity away. Rather than learn from their successful limited-government counterparts, they often instead seek to spread the misery, to suppress the natural competition that successful states—those that believe in the power of the people over the power of government—represent.

Federal politicians have already proven they do not have the wisdom, will, or courage to say no to these liberal-progressive states and to the unions, trial lawyers, and other special interests that want to impose their misguided ideas and values on the entire country.

There is hope, though. As more conservative, free-market states show their citizens through experience that limited-government ideas preserve liberty and create success and prosperity, there is hope that Americans will demand the same proven and principled approach to governing at the federal level. And as Ken and his fellow attorneys general keep fighting continuing federal overreach, they are making more citizens aware of the threat such overreach poses to their personal and economic freedom, eventually leading them to the conclusion that they need to change their elected representatives in Washington if they are to change the direction of their country.

CHAPTER 1

THE BIGGEST SET OF
LAWBREAKERS IN AMERICA

||||||||||||||||||||||||||||||||||||||||||||||||||||||||||||||||||||||||||||||||||||||||||||||||||||||

There is but one element of government, and that is the people . . .
For a nation to be free, it is only necessary that she wills it. For
a nation to be slave, it is only necessary that she wills it.

—JOHN ADAMS, 1814, Founding Father and
second president of the United States

IN MARCH 2010, President Barack Obama and the Democrat-controlled 111th Congress did to the American people what the tyrant we rebelled against in 1775 couldn't even do when we were merely subjects: they declared that they suddenly had the unprecedented power to force Americans to purchase private products in the name of whatever "public good" the federal government deemed appropriate.

In March 2010, that product was private health insurance, and the mandate to buy it was the centerpiece of the new federal health care law, the Patient Protection and Affordable Care Act, also dubbed Obamacare.

But this new power Congress and the president claimed for themselves had the potential to go far beyond the ability to force Americans to purchase just health insurance. The power could be used to force them to buy cars to prop up the ailing automobile industry, to buy gym memberships and vegetables to promote healthy lifestyles, or to buy

1

virtually anything for whatever Congress and the president declared was the public good.

By passing the Patient Protection and Affordable Care Act (PPACA) with this individual insurance mandate, Congress and the president had violated the United States Constitution, as no such power to mandate private purchases had ever been given to the federal government. Unfortunately, without enough lawmakers in Congress willing to uphold their oath to "support and defend the Constitution of the United States" and vote *against* the unconstitutional act, it became law, and it fell to people like me and my fellow state attorneys general to take the federal government to court to attempt to stop its overreach. In other words, the states had to sue the federal government to protect the U.S. Constitution and our citizens *from* the federal government.

Though a mandate was unconstitutional, many Americans would embrace this newfound federal power to seemingly solve yet one more of our society's challenges: health insurance that was too expensive and out of the reach of too many people. Fortunately, the majority of Americans saw this new mandate power for what it was: a diminishing of our liberty that would be difficult to undo, and a power that could just as easily be used for not-so-altruistic purposes down the road.

This book attempts to chronicle the courtroom and the behind-the-scenes fight against one of the greatest assaults on American liberty in our lifetimes—the federal health insurance mandate. I'll also cover other lawless acts of what I call the biggest set of lawbreakers in America—the Obama administration. No other president, no other administration has had such a willful disregard for the law.

The administration used its temporary majority in Congress as well as executive branch agencies like the Environmental Protection Agency (EPA), the Federal Communications Commission (FCC), and others to exercise control over the American people that it didn't have the authority to exercise, and in the process, it trampled the sovereignty of the states, violated federal law, ignored federal courts, and violated the Constitution to achieve its goals of redistributing wealth, concentrating power in Washington, and rewarding its political allies.

Although I had many policy disagreements with the health care law and the other federal actions I'll describe throughout this book, I won't get into many policy discussions here, because that's already been done elsewhere and because—as the attorney general of Virginia—I couldn't sue the federal government just because I didn't like its policies.

We Americans had seen our share of bad laws from Washington that punished achievers, harmed one class of people to advantage another, or ravaged the economy to put more power in the hands of government. But just because laws were bad policy and went against the principles of small government didn't necessarily mean they were unconstitutional. For instance, I had said all along during Virginia's lawsuit against Obamacare that if the federal health care law had been passed in a constitutional way—funded with a legal tax on citizens instead of as an unconstitutional mandate to buy a private product—I would have had no authority to sue. Fighting back on bad policy is the role of Congress and the people. If laws are onerous but constitutional, the only remedy is at the ballot box—by electing new members of Congress and a new president.

However, when the president is willing to *ignore the law* repeatedly or *disregard the Constitution* to force his radical policies on the American people and the states, state attorneys general like me are able to step up and push back in the courts.

H ow did this fight with the federal government come about? To best answer this question, we need to refer back to the history of the United States—starting all the way back with the country's founding.

3

In 1775, American colonists began to fight what initially seemed like a futile revolution to throw off the shackles of a powerful tyrant and struggle for their independence. Against the odds, they freed themselves from Great Britain and created a government of their own—one that would exist to secure and protect their newly won liberty.

The framers of the Constitution started with the premise that the government would derive its powers from the people and ultimately would answer to them. They painstakingly designed the Constitution—the document that created the federal government—to grant the government only *limited* powers, because they understood that a strong central government would be a constant threat to the cherished liberty they had recently won. Regrettably, in the centuries since the Constitution was adopted, we as a people have demanded that government do more to "fix" society's problems—from poverty to high food costs to transportation issues—and to accommodate those demands, government has willingly grown beyond its original mandate.

We have ended up relying more on government and less on ourselves, our families, our churches, our friends, and our communities. With every new societal problem, enterprising politicians—backed by a cavalcade of cronies and special interests—have identified a new government program or agency to solve it. In the process, the principles of limited government have been pushed aside for what some deemed "the greater good." If the new program was unconstitutional or violated the law, well, then, they declared, that just meant the Constitution or the law wasn't able to keep up with the times.

Few seemed to notice the cost of these solutions—not just in dollars, but in *liberty*. Every time we asked government to do something new, we had to transfer some of our authority to it to allow the government to carry out those solutions. Every transfer of our authority came at the expense of just a little more of our liberty. Bit by bit, our federal government gained more and more power, while the people retained less and less.

We had long forgotten Thomas Jefferson's admonition that "eternal vigilance is the price of liberty." We weren't very vigilant, and we let people like President Obama's former chief of staff, Rahm "you never want a serious crisis to go to waste" Emanuel, use real and perceived crises to convince people to let government grow its power at every opportunity.

Of course, President Obama wasn't the only one who was to blame for accumulating so much power to the federal government to so thoroughly trample our liberty. That process had been a steady *bipartisan* march for more than the last one hundred years of American government.

The government's growth of power over those years ultimately set the stage for 2009: Under the Obama administration, with a willing president, the government shifted from *deriving* its authority from the people to *seizing* authority from the people. The administration circumvented Congress to unilaterally change immigration law, defied a federal court order to regulate the Internet, bypassed the authority of the states to try to put the coal industry out of business, and worked with Congress to violate the Constitution to push mandatory health insurance on all its citizens.

We were finally confronting head-on the big-government leviathan President Gerald Ford had warned us about when he said, "A government big enough to give you everything you need, is a government big enough to take away everything that you have."

This was exactly what our founders had feared. As a result of massive government growth, we had a government that existed to plan and control virtually every aspect of our lives and our economy, from energy to automobiles to banking, insurance, and health care. We had a government so large, powerful, and costly that not only was our liberty at stake, but so were our financial freedom and our very way of life.

But something remarkable also started happening in 2009 to counter all that. As our founders once did against a tyrant king, citizens and states began to push back against the federal government in an attempt to stop its out-of-control growth. As the government borrowed hundreds of billions of dollars from the Communist Chinese to bail out failed U.S. financial institutions, car companies, and American home-owners who were encouraged to buy houses they couldn't afford, tax-payers started to get angry. And as talk of putting the American health care industry under government control became actual legislation working its way through Congress, citizens started to protest. Many organized, and the Tea Party movement—named in honor of the 1773 Boston Tea Party rebellion against the British Crown—emerged.

In February 2009, just weeks before the national Tea Party move-ment started to take shape, *Newsweek* ran an editorial by then-editor Jon Meacham titled "We Are All Socialists Now." The editorial cap-tured the American people's frustration that government spending was growing at an unsustainable pace and government control of the American economy was unparalleled compared with any other time in our history. It also spoke to their frustration that it wasn't only Presi-dent Obama and a Democrat-controlled Congress that had caused it all, but that the previous Republican administration and Republican Congress—those whom they had expected to put the brakes on gov-ernment expansion—had actually had their feet on the big-govern-ment accelerator, too:

> In many ways our economy already resembles a European one. As boomers age and spending grows, we will become even more French. . . . The U.S. government has already—under a conservative Republican [President George W. Bush's] administration—effectively nationalized the bank-ing and mortgage industries [with hundreds of billions of dollars in taxpayer-funded industry bailouts]. . . .
>
> [B]ut it was, again, under a conservative GOP admin-

istration that we enacted the largest expansion of the welfare state in 30 years: prescription drugs for the elderly . . . And it is unlikely that even the reddest of states will decline federal money for infrastructural improvements. . . .

Whether we like it or not—or even whether many people have thought much about it or not—the numbers clearly suggest that we are headed in a more European direction. A decade ago U.S. government spending was 34.3 percent of GDP, compared with 48.2 percent in the euro zone—a roughly 14-point gap, according to the Organisation for Economic Co-operation and Development. In 2010 U.S. spending is expected to be 39.9 percent of GDP, compared with 47.1 percent in the euro zone—a gap of less than 8 points. As entitlement spending rises over the next decade, we will become even more French.

It was this sense of America's inevitable slide toward socialism that finally moved average citizens to organize into the Tea Party movement and become skeptical of both Republican and Democrat politicians. They started to take more of an interest in their government, educate themselves about politics, and even study the history of our Founding Fathers.

In all my years in politics, I had never seen such an interest in the Constitution and our founding principles as I saw emerge in 2009 with the Tea Party movement. I used to think I was one of only a small group of people who even read the Constitution and tried to abide by it, but it's now commonplace to hear average citizens talk about the Constitution and limited-government principles in political discussions.

The American people had been asleep, letting their power go and their government grow. The Tea Party movement reawakened them to the fact that they could no longer take their freedom for granted. It also warned of what was to come if they didn't do something to change course soon.

As a result, citizens started to take notice of what their elected officials were voting for. People began to study the Constitution to learn the legal limits of government authority. Protests in Washington and at congressional district offices and town halls across the country became the order of the day.

In the so-called summer of discontent in 2009, politicians were forced to start paying attention to their constituents a lot more. And the states started to realize that they weren't wholly owned subsidiaries of U.S. Congress, Inc., ready and willing to carry out the orders of a Congress and a president whose actions were unconstitutional or contrary to the law.

It was in that tumult of 2009 that I was elected Virginia's attorney general. While I took on the typical duties of a state attorney general, on the day I was sworn into office, like every other state and federal elected official, I also swore an oath to defend the Constitution of the United States. That's an oath I took very seriously, even if others thought such an attitude was passé.

So when the federal government went so far as to disregard the law or overstep the bounds of its constitutional authority in such a way as to harm the Commonwealth of Virginia in the process, I had the legal authority to push back in court. And I did.

In fact, this was precisely the system that the framers of the Constitution had set up to keep the federal government in check. Just as the framers divided the power of the federal government among the legislative, executive, and judicial branches in a system of checks and balances to ensure each branch served as a watchdog over the others, so too did they divide authority for governing between the federal government and the state governments—a concept called federalism. Federalism is another level of checks and balances that allows the states to serve as a fail-safe to prevent the federal government from becoming so powerful that it becomes destructive of the very liberty it was instituted to protect. Remember "[to] secure the Blessings of Liberty to ourselves and our posterity" in the Preamble of the Constitution?

It was in this spirit of federalism—the idea of the states standing up to the federal government when it overstepped its legal or constitutional bounds—that Virginia and eventually twenty-seven other states decided to file suit over the 2010 health care act. I'm not aware of any other time in American history when so many states were plaintiffs against the federal government, attempting to rein in its power. It was a truly historical and critical test for our constitutional republic.

Virginia was the first state in the nation to get to federal court and argue that the new health care law was unconstitutional. Our legal argument was that the government's attempt to use the clause in the Constitution that allowed Congress to regulate interstate commerce didn't allow Congress to *order* people *into* commerce to purchase private health insurance. The federal government could tax you, but it didn't have the power to force you to purchase something.

There was a reason there had never been a mandate like this in all of American history: for the 234 years prior to 2010, everyone had known that the federal government lacked the power to do it.

Interestingly, in the 1760s, when we were still subjects under British rule, the American colonists refused to buy British goods to protest several new taxes imposed by Parliament. King George III viewed the boycotts as illegal, even treasonous. But the king's own lawyers—the attorney general and the solicitor general—told Parliament that the boycotts were *legal* under British law. That answer was a concession that the king and Parliament couldn't order their own subjects to purchase British goods.

Imagine the irony in 2010 when the president and Congress

ordered free American *citizens* to do what the tyrant we rebelled against acknowledged that even he didn't have the authority to do when we were merely *subjects*. As I said, the reason there had never been a mandate like this before in American history is because everyone knew the government lacked the power to do it—everyone, that is, except President Barack Obama and the Democrat-controlled 111th Congress.

Americans may disagree on what the different parts of the Constitution mean and on the acceptable size of government, but those who know even a little history must agree that we established a government that was supposed to be less powerful than the one from which we declared our independence.

Forcing citizens into commerce to buy government-approved health insurance sounded more like what governments did to *subjects*, not to citizens. And that's why I said from day one of our health care challenge that our lawsuit wasn't about health care; it was about *liberty*.

THE HEALTH CARE case was just one of the fronts in the states' fights against the federal government's lawbreaking. Even before the health care suit, Virginia, Texas, Alabama, and several other states were pushing back against the federal Environmental Protection Agency—or what I like to call the Employment Prevention Agency (as that seems to be what it does best these days).

In 2009, the EPA used discredited and politicized data it borrowed from the United Nations to declare that carbon dioxide and other greenhouse gases like methane were pollutants dangerous to public health because they allegedly caused global warming. Yet carbon dioxide is what we exhale every second of every day. It keeps the trees alive and allows them to make the oxygen that keeps *us* alive. It's a wonderful symbiotic system that sustains life on earth.

But to environmentalists, carbon dioxide is a slow killer. And by declaring it a pollutant, the EPA could regulate its emission from everything from power-generating plants, to factories and office buildings, to individual cars and trucks. In other words, with this single declaration, the EPA was able to put a massive part of the U.S. economy under its control under the guise of stopping global warming.

In assuming this new authority, this agency of mass destruction was able to foist on America a job-killing, economy-killing regulatory scheme that Congress had already considered but had refused to pass. In other words, since President Obama couldn't get the votes in Congress to pass legislation capping carbon dioxide emissions (because so many Americans opposed it), he decided to have one of his executive branch agencies implement the policy instead.

This EPA scheme will eventually allow the agency to impose strict and often unattainable limits (under any current or emerging technology) on carbon dioxide emissions. Whole industries will have to either spend billions to retool to meet the emissions standards, pay heavy fines, close, or move overseas.

That won't just cost jobs. It will eventually cost every American household thousands of dollars a year in increased energy bills and increased costs for everything that takes energy to manufacture or to transport: food, clothing, appliances, furniture, and more.

I got involved and filed suit when, in its zealous rush to create this new and unprecedented power for itself, the EPA broke the law by shortcutting its own procedures and policies. It borrowed foreign data when it was supposed to do its own research—or *at least* verify the accuracy of what it had borrowed.

When Virginia and Texas and a number of other parties asked the EPA to go back through the process and do it right, and it refused, we asked the courts to compel the agency to do so.

As of this writing, the case is still in the courts.

We should all be alarmed whenever the government creates regulations that will have such an enormous impact on the American economy and our standard of living but refuses to comply with its own rules to ensure the accuracy of the data that underlies its decision.

But as alarming as that was, the Obama administration's overreach and willful disregard for the law didn't stop with health care or the EPA.

The administration, in a further attempt to appease extreme environmentalists, also tried to shut down coal mining in Virginia, West Virginia, Kentucky, and other coal states by choking off the issuance of mining permits.

In 2011, the federal Office of Surface Mining Reclamation and Enforcement—the OSM, an obscure executive agency under the president—created aggressive new directives to interfere with states' issuance of coal mining permits in an attempt to overrule the oversight authority of states. The problem was that the OSM's newly "discovered" authority had never been authorized by Congress. In fact, since the 1970s, Congress had given states the *exclusive* responsibility to regulate surface mining within their own borders, and nothing in the law had changed since then.

The meaning of the word *exclusive* had even been litigated in court before. (If you want to know how that one ended, it was with *exclusive* meaning exactly what you think it means!) And yet the feds pressed on . . .

This overreach by the OSM was clearly illegal, in defiance of Congress, and a usurpation of state authority.

Unfortunately, I can't say that I was surprised. During his presidential campaign, then-senator Obama had said unabashedly that he wanted to put the coal industry out of business. He felt it was too harmful for the environment for the government to continue to "let" the industry exist, despite the fact that coal provides nearly half of all electricity for the United States, as well as jobs for some of the poorest areas of the country. The OSM's move showed that this promise to bankrupt the coal industry was a promise the president was intent on keeping.

But the overreach didn't stop there. On the labor front, Virginia worked with South Carolina attorney general Alan Wilson and more than a dozen other state attorneys general to take on the National Labor Relations Board (NLRB) when it tried to sanction a private company for building a manufacturing plant in a state that *didn't require* workers to join the union to get a job with the company. The NLRB charged the Boeing Company with unfair labor practices for simply setting up a factory in the right-to-work state of South Carolina instead of expanding its unionized plant in Washington.

In right-to-work states, workers can't be forced to join labor unions as a condition of employment—it's the workers' choice to join unions. In non-right-to-work states, the law says join the union or don't get the job.

In reality, the labor board's complaint against Boeing was just blatant favoritism by Obama-appointed board members to Democrat-leaning unions. The complaint showed a total disregard for the facts and the law and was a not-so-veiled assault on the ability of twenty-three right-to-work states to recruit industry and create new jobs. It was also the government's very open attempt to intimidate companies from doing business in right-to-work states—often states that also happen to have Republican voter majorities. And perhaps most critical to average Americans: because this was a threat against companies that tried to create jobs where union membership wasn't compulsory, it was an outright assault on a citizen's right to work without being forced to join a union.

But as bad as the attempts to unilaterally destroy part of the energy industry and intimidate job creators were, one of most egregious overreaches came from the Obama Federal Communications Commission when it attempted to regulate the Internet by imposing so-called net neutrality regulations on Internet service providers *in direct defiance of a federal court ruling.*

The principle of net neutrality states that the federal government should mandate that broadband Internet service providers (the companies that bring high-speed Internet into our homes) let all data flow at the same speed and charge all consumers the same price, regardless of how much of the Internet pipeline each consumer uses.

I'll get into more detail on net neutrality in a later chapter, but the point is that, from a legal perspective, there was a very big problem with what the FCC did. A federal court had *already* told the agency that it had absolutely no authority to regulate the Internet. But the FCC *defied* that order and attempted to move forward with regulations anyway.

An agency's refusal to honor a federal court order was a new low for lawbreaking, and it posed a serious threat to our representative form of government. If the federal government was not only willing to break the law but then wasn't willing to stop breaking the law when a court ordered it to, how could we ever expect the government to respect the laws that protected the rights of citizens?

The bottom line was that the Obama administration aggressively used administrative agencies like the EPA, the NLRB, the OSM, and the FCC and their unelected bureaucrats to accomplish policy objectives that the people's elected representatives in Congress wouldn't even approve. President Obama and his appointees time and again ignored any limit to their power that they found inconvenient—federal laws, binding rulings of federal courts, and the Constitution—all to make government work in ways they couldn't achieve through the democratic process.

Unfortunately, we didn't have a majority of our representatives in Washington who were willing to uphold their oath to the Constitution to stop these assaults. So state attorneys general—once known mostly for suing companies to protect consumers—joined forces and became known for suing the federal government to *protect liberty*.

We unexpectedly became the last line of defense against an overreaching, lawbreaking federal government.

We were there to fight. And we didn't just pick the fights we knew we could win. We picked the fights that needed to be fought. As a result, we didn't always win every legal battle. But even when we lost, whenever we very vocally fought for principles, we *still* won, because in the process, we educated people through media coverage, town halls, and even Rotary meetings. And when we reached them, we awakened their resolve to take up the fight with us so we could come back in even stronger numbers to fight another day.

Yes, there was value in fighting, even when winning wasn't certain. Founding Father Patrick Henry lost when he argued that the Constitution shouldn't be adopted because it created a national government that was too powerful. But it was precisely because he refused to back down after that loss that we ultimately got the Bill of Rights, which has been indispensable in protecting our liberties ever since.

Slowly, my colleagues and I shifted the paradigm for what was expected of Republican state attorneys general. When I was elected, Texas was the only state I knew of that had some kind of standard review of laws and regulations that were considered federalism threats. We adopted that model in Virginia and put such scrutiny on steroids.

As the Obama administration continued its overreach and pushed against the states and the people, Republican candidates for attorney general across the country either started running for office on a federalism platform or soon joined our fight after being elected: Luther Strange in Alabama, Alan Wilson in South Carolina, Pam Bondi in Florida, Bill Schuette in Michigan, Tom Horne in Arizona, and Sam Olens in Georgia. In 2010, a candidate for attorney general in Oklahoma, Scott Pruitt, would run—and *win*—on a platform of actually

15

establishing a *federalism unit* within the Oklahoma attorney general's office to combat "systematic overreach by federal agencies, boards and offices." As each candidate won his or her election, more states joined in the fight.

Tom Horne challenged the constitutionality of Section 5 of the Voting Rights Act, which required certain states to get the federal government's blessing on any changes to state voting procedures, no matter how trivial; Luther Strange, Alan Wilson, and Tom Horne sued to allow their states to enforce federal immigration laws to stem the tide of illegal immigration; Greg Abbott in Texas and others fought the job-killing EPA when it continued to mandate oppressive and illegal regulations with little environmental benefit; Alan Wilson fought against the National Labor Relations Board's attempt to threaten the future of nonunionized jobs; and of course, twenty-eight of us challenged the federal health care law.

Federalism—a term rarely used by anyone other than academics and a concept rarely considered by the states—started to gain major traction. Federalism was reborn in America and would soon become the primary force to rein the federal government back inside the bounds of the Constitution and the law. Very quickly, Washington politicians knew that the states and the American people would no longer stand idly by and watch their liberties be taken away.

I N THE FOLLOWING pages of this book, I'll detail each of these battles and others we and the other states had with the federal government. I'll cover the tremendous audacity of the president, certain members of Congress, and the federal bureaucrats who grabbed more control for Washington, regardless of what the law or the Constitution authorized them to do.

I'll explain what happened in each of these battles and give you an insider's view of some of the behind-the-scenes strategies we used to push back, as well as the federal government's often absurd reasoning for doing what it did. I'll detail the attempts by some in the media to willingly propagandize for the administration to lull Americans into thinking government was just doing what was best for the people, regardless of the toll it would take on American liberty.

As an aside, I want to state early on that I take many in the media to task in this book: those who deliberately distorted the truth in their stories (okay, this is a euphemism; actually, they outright lied), those who only told half the facts (the facts that supported their world view), those who advocated for big government regardless of the consequences, and those who couldn't help but be openly hostile in their interviews with me.

But I also want to recognize that there are some terrific reporters and editors that I've had the privilege of working with who truly report the news in a straightforward way. For most of those reporters and editors, I couldn't tell you their political leanings, or even if they have any—and that's a compliment to them. With their fair and factual reporting, they are doing what our Founding Fathers envisioned: informing the public and providing needed scrutiny and accountability to government.

In this book, I'll also take you back to 1776 and examine the principles of our founding and why those principles of liberty and limited government aren't outdated relics of the past, hindering our progress toward Utopia—although that's what the big-government statists would have us believe. I'll explain how those principles work to guarantee your freedom and why they are as timeless and as important today as they were in 1776. I hope that this book will help more people appreciate what an amazing gift of freedom we have in this country so they'll be less willing to vote for politicians who are eager to take that gift away from us.

I'll also introduce you to some people who say the Constitution is no longer relevant, including some of our most influential members of the media. They accuse our Founding Fathers of having no ability to conceive of the issues we would face today, such as skyrocketing health care costs, energy issues, or the revolution of the Internet. What those people forget is that the founders intimately understood tyranny. And they created a constitution to limit government—precisely to keep that government from accumulating the kind of tyrannical power they rebelled against.

The founders did that to ensure that the generations that followed them would forever live as citizens, and never again as subjects.

CHAPTER 2

A PEOPLE WHO HAD FORGOTTEN
THEIR OWN HISTORY

|||||||||||||||||||||||||||||||||||||||||||||||||||||||||||||||||||||||||||||||||||||||||||||||||||||||||||||||||||||

Not too long ago, two friends of mine were talking to a Cuban
refugee, a businessman who had escaped from Castro, and in the
midst of his story one of my friends turned to the other and said,
"We don't know how lucky we are." And the Cuban stopped and
said, "How lucky you are? I had someplace to escape to." And in
that sentence he told us the entire story. If we lose freedom here,
there's no place to escape to. This is the last stand on earth.

—Ronald Reagan, in "A Time for Choosing," his televised
speech during the 1964 U.S. presidential election campaign

WHY DOES THE Constitution—written more than two hundred
years ago by "a bunch of dead white guys," as its modern detractors like to tell us—still matter in the twenty-first century? What
were the states fighting for when they challenged the federal government over the first steps toward nationalized health care, when they
challenged the EPA over its new power to shut down entire industries, and when they challenged the National Labor Relations Board
for sanctioning companies that opened nonunionized manufacturing
plants?

The states were fighting to preserve the rule of law. If the government were allowed to break the law without challenge, how could

Americans ever again feel secure that the law would protect their liberty?

No place else on earth has the degree of individual liberty that the United States does, and that's because we've limited government's power so government exists to serve the people; the people do not exist to serve the government. For this reason, limited government should be important to all of us—Democrat, Republican, liberal, conservative, libertarian, or vegetarian—because constitutionally limited government prevents tyranny. This model has allowed the American people to create a nation where free people, free markets, faith, education, family, prosperity, business, innovation, security, lawfulness, and patriotism can all thrive.

The Constitution with its Bill of Rights is not a code of laws for citizens; it is the law that *governs government*. The Constitution is the blueprint that established what few things the federal government is allowed to do and how it is to do them. It isn't just a set of aspirational thoughts about how government *should* act. It is the law that guides how government *must* act. Any law the federal government passes, any order the president issues, and any decision a federal court makes are supposed to fall within the limits of the Constitution. Just as laws restrain individuals from harming one another, the Constitution restrains the government from harming the individual and his liberty.

The Constitution governs how our laws are made, how they are executed and enforced, and how they are adjudicated in the courts. When the Constitution is violated—when it's corrupted by the very people who swore oaths to uphold it—our entire system of governance, of laws, and of justice is thereby corrupted.

If the government chooses to ignore one part of the Constitution or the law for political expediency—even if it's for something many people feel is a "good cause," such as health care "for everyone"— then what happens when government chooses to ignore other parts, such as our right to free speech, our right to freely associate with others, our right to trial by jury and due process, or our right to be free from illegal searches and seizures?

You don't have to look very far to see what it's like to live without limits on government authority. Look at Cuba, just ninety miles off America's shore, where men and women are jailed and tortured if they speak out against the government, jobs are assigned by the state, and government permission is required to move to a different home; or North Korea, where perceived enemies of the state are denied work and subject to starvation, and citizens are required to spy on one another and attend weekly indoctrination sessions; or China, where couples aren't allowed to have more than one child and mothers who violate local family planning regulations are forced to have abortions or sterilizations, and where all religious organizations not registered and approved by the government are illegal, with members risking fines and criminal prosecution.

There are no limits on the power of these governments; thus Cubans, North Koreans, and the Chinese exist to serve their governments, instead of their governments existing to serve them.

Unfortunately, there are many influential big-government advocates in America who think authoritarian rule is really just a more efficient way to get things done (just be sure to look the other way when there's religious persecution, forced sterilization, or imprisonment for speaking out against the government). And even more regrettable is that such statists—who have no use for the Constitution or the rule of law—are sprinkled throughout all levels of government and media.

Take, for example, *New York Times* columnist Thomas Friedman. In a 2009 column, he wrote longingly of China:

> Watching both the health care and climate/energy debates in Congress, it is hard not to draw the following

conclusion: There is only one thing worse than one-party autocracy, and that is one-party democracy, which is what we have in America today.

One-party autocracy certainly has its drawbacks. But when it is led by a reasonably enlightened group of people, as China is today, it can also have great advantages.

Yes, one-party autocracy has great advantages, like the lack of free-speech protections, the Tiananmen Square Massacre of unarmed protesters, and home visits by government officials to keep citizens "in line."

Friedman's comments weren't just a slip of the pen, because in a 2010 appearance on NBC's *Meet the Press* with host Tom Brokaw just weeks before President Obama signed Obamacare into law, Friedman said it again when he opined that the democratic process would get us a less-than-optimal health care reform law:

> [Y]ou know, I've been saying for a while, Tom, there's only one thing worse than one-party autocracy—the Chinese form of government—and that's one-party democracy. You know, in China, if the leadership can get around to an enlightened decision, it can order it from the top down, okay.
>
> Here [in the United States], when you have one-party democracy, one party ruling—basically the other party just basically saying no—every solution is sub-optimal. You know, and when your chief competitor in the world can order optimal and you can only produce sub-optimal?

Sure, who wouldn't trade freedom for efficiency? I understand the Chinese people are just thrilled with the trade-off.

God save us from Thomas Friedman's "optimal America."

The Founding Fathers Were Imperfect

BEFORE I WRITE any further about the Founding Fathers and the framers of the Constitution (a subgroup of the founders), I want to make one point so that no one accuses me of distorting the record of these men and their fallibility. The Founding Fathers were far from perfect, and the sin of slavery was the most obvious example of that.

They were intensely divided over the issue. John Jay was one of many who detested the institution, and he summed up the hypocrisy of fighting for American independence and declaring that "all men are created equal" while still allowing slavery to exist when he said simply, "To contend for our own liberty, and to deny that blessing to others, involves an inconsistency not to be excused."

Many tried to rid the early United States of slavery but were unsuccessful. But the fact that the institution and other injustices existed didn't mean the founding principles were wrong; it meant, unfortunately, that not all the founders lived up to the principles they advocated.

We all know the founders weren't perfect, but the principles they espoused of life, liberty, and equality under the law, and of a government of limited powers to protect those principles, always will be.

The Federal Government's Power Was Meant to Be Limited

THE DECLARATION OF INDEPENDENCE clearly laid out the founders' vision that people had inherent rights that could not be taken away by any earthly power: "All men are created equal, that they are endowed by their Creator with certain unalienable Rights."

It also explained that a government would be created to protect these rights from foreign and domestic infringements: "That to secure these rights, Governments are instituted among Men." Without some sort of government and a set of laws, people couldn't be secure in their rights and would live in fear of foreign invaders and domestic criminals.

The Declaration also stated that government was granted its power *by the people,* and therefore, was under *their* control, not the other way around: "deriving their just powers from the consent of the governed."

The philosophy of the majority of the Founding Fathers was that, other than handling defense, foreign affairs, and a few domestic issues, the federal government generally was supposed to stay out of the affairs of the people and let them flourish in their liberty, which it was charged with protecting. The remaining governing would be left to the states (being closer to the people) and to the people themselves.

We know a great deal about the intent of the framers of the Constitution from a collection of eighty-five essays called the *Federalist Papers,* which were written by James Madison, Alexander Hamilton, and John Jay to convince the people of New York to direct their delegates to ratify the Constitution. With regard to the limited powers of the federal government, James Madison said in *Federalist No. 45:*

> The powers delegated by the proposed Constitution to the federal government, are few and defined. Those which are to remain in the State governments are numerous and indefinite. The former will be exercised principally on external objects, as war, peace, negotiation, and foreign commerce; with which last the power of taxation will, for the most part, be connected. The powers reserved to the several States will extend to all the objects which, in the ordinary course of affairs, concern the lives, liberties, and properties of the people, and the internal order, improvement, and prosperity of the State.

Since the federal government's only way to achieve anything was through the force of law (the key word here being *force*), the founders didn't want it micromanaging the people and all of their affairs—even for the purpose of some perceived noble goal—because it would inevitably infringe on the right of the people to simply be left alone. As Thomas Jefferson prescribed in his first inaugural address in 1801:

> A wise and frugal government . . . shall restrain men from injuring one another, shall leave them otherwise free to regulate their own pursuits of industry and improvement, and shall not take from the mouth of labor the bread it has earned. This is the sum of good government.

To prevent the federal government from exceeding its authority, the framers built several "fail-safes" into the Constitution, five of which I'll discuss here.

One fail-safe was to specifically list, or enumerate, the powers of the government and to limit its authority to only those powers, reserving all other powers to the people and the states. Another fail-safe was to later create a bill of rights—a list of the rights of the people that the government couldn't infringe upon. A third was to separate the government's powers, not only by dividing them among the three branches of government (the executive, legislative, and judicial), but also by dividing the Congress into a house and a senate, and by dividing the governing powers between the federal and state governments. A fourth fail-safe was the ability to impeach and remove government officials from office for treason, bribery, or other "high Crimes and Misdemeanors."

Finally, a fifth fail-safe was to create a representative form of government in which the people and the states elected the president and members of Congress, so that those in power held their jobs only as long as the people and the states approved (note that prior to the Seventeenth Amendment, state legislatures elected U.S. senators).

Many laws that Congress passes and that the president signs might tax us excessively, might be terrible policy, and might infringe on our liberty, but they might not necessarily be unconstitutional. With this fifth fail-safe, the Constitution protects our liberties by letting the American people fire congressmen and presidents who make bad laws and replace them with people they think will do a better job. This preserves the people as the ultimate sovereigns—the ones who possess the supreme political power.

Why the Separation of Powers?

THE SEPARATION OF powers among the three branches, the two houses of Congress, and the states is meant to neutralize any concentration of power in one entity and allows each to have competing interests in preserving its own authority. If one particular branch or level of government oversteps its bounds and infringes on the power of one of the others, the other can exercise its powers in retaliation. That way, each branch serves as a check and balance on the power of the others, and the states and the federal government serve as checks on each other.

As I stated in chapter 1, this division of powers that creates a system of checks and balances between the federal government and the state governments is called federalism.

Even Founding Father Alexander Hamilton—not necessarily an enthusiastic advocate of small government—saw the need to divide power between the federal and state governments. At the New York convention to ratify the Constitution, he said:

> This balance between the National and State governments ought to be dwelt on with peculiar attention, as it is of the utmost importance. It forms a double security

to the people. If one encroaches on their rights they will find a powerful protection in the other. Indeed, they will both be prevented from overpassing their constitutional limits by a certain rivalship, which will ever subsist between them.

This dual sovereignty served our nation well when the federal government had to step up in the 1950s and '60s to enforce the civil rights of black citizens when states were violating them. In the 2010s, this dual sovereignty served the nation again, but in reverse, as the states challenged the federal government in an effort to push it back within its constitutional bounds and stop its lawbreaking.

Why were the states given so much power in our federal system? The most obvious reason was the one I just stated: to provide a check on federal power. There were other reasons, but let's discuss just a few of the biggest. First, it was the *states* (the thirteen original colonies) that were the impetus for creating the federal government, not the other way around.

Second, the founders felt that state governments were closer to the people geographically and politically, and the people could more easily and effectively petition their state legislators than they could the federal government.

Third, the bulk of governing was expected to be done at the state level.

Fourth, the federal government was just too big to impose one-size-fits-all laws on many aspects of American life. The states would be what were later termed "laboratories of democracy," competing with each other for that right mix of government that was big enough to serve the people yet not so powerful that it was a threat to individual liberty. In the end, this set-up permitted people to vote with their feet and move to states that were governed better, which could drive the states that were losing population to improve.

In this day and age of such an all-powerful federal government, many people don't remember that it was important for the states to be a check on Washington's power. There are some people who see the states pushing back against the federal government in recent years as extreme. Either out of ignorance or out of a desire for un-chained government expansion, they say that no one can challenge the power of the feds. *But that's exactly what the framers of the Constitution intended!*

The Bill of Rights

EVEN AS THE Constitution was being written, debates centered on the fear that the new federal government would be too powerful, especially the Office of the President, which some felt would devolve into a monarchy. Many people, led by Patrick Henry, wanted to defeat ratification of the Constitution altogether.

Debates also ensued about whether a written guarantee of the rights of citizens should be included in the Constitution. Those who felt that the government might not stick to its constitutional compact rallied for a bill of rights during the Constitution's ratification process.

James Madison was one who felt that such a bill of rights wasn't necessary, and he vehemently argued that the framers had created a constitution that sufficiently restricted the federal government to a list of very *specific* and *limited* powers of which it *could not act outside*. He felt that by default, all other authority and rights remained with the states and the people and that the government didn't have any pow-ers not *explicitly* granted to it. (Oops! Apparently he didn't anticipate politicians and courts reading "between the lines" of the Constitution to give themselves all sorts of new powers over the next two-hundred-plus years.)

The opponents of a bill of rights had another fairly convincing argument as well. They felt it would be impossible to list all the people's rights, as they were almost indefinite, and they were concerned that writing a definitive list would imply that those were the *only* rights the people retained, which was never their intent.

The debate came to a head in Virginia's constitutional ratification convention in June 1788. The pro-ratification side, led by James Madison, always knew that Patrick Henry would be their most difficult foe to overcome. And for more than three hot weeks in Richmond, the two sides debated, shouted, whispered, and schemed to scrape together the votes to win Virginia, as all the states knew the Constitution couldn't work without the commonwealth's buy-in.

Patrick Henry's opposition to the Constitution and push to at least include a bill of rights to safeguard the people proved to be a powerful influence. Although Mr. Madison was not in favor, to get the votes needed for ratification, he bowed to political necessity and promised that in the first session of the new Congress, he would pursue amendments to the Constitution that would protect individual liberties like the right to worship, free speech, free association, and property rights. His commitment to support a bill of rights won over enough convention delegates for ratification to prevail—89 to 79—with Patrick Henry, George Mason, and future president James Monroe voting against the new blueprint for the federal government.

An even thinner margin occurred in New York a month later, with a 31–29 vote in favor of ratification. The Constitution was only ratified in New York because of a similar expectation that a bill of rights would be added.

When Mr. Madison was later elected to Congress, he kept his word and helped get the Bill of Rights ratified as the first ten amendments to the Constitution.

Patrick Henry's hard-fought effort is a lesson for everyone who fights for principles. The lesson is that we don't always win on the first round, but that doesn't mean we go home and stop trying. Mr. Henry won while losing. In 1788, he lost the battle to stop the ratification of the Constitution and its creation of a strong federal government. But he didn't stop fighting, and in 1791, despite the challenges and the nay-sayers, he got what he had been working for: he had won for all future generations the written protection of their core liberties. And aren't we grateful today for his persistence? Look how often court cases are decided on First Amendment, Fourth Amendment, and Fifth Amendment grounds, and on other rights listed in those first ten amendments.

To address the concerns that creating a definitive list of rights would imply that those were the only rights the people retained, the Ninth and Tenth Amendments were included in the Bill of Rights. The Ninth Amendment states that though the Bill of Rights contains a list of certain rights that are guaranteed to the people, a partial list was never meant to be construed as denying other God-given rights:

> The enumeration in the Constitution, of certain rights, shall not be construed to deny or disparage others retained by the people.

The Tenth Amendment clarified in plain English that the powers *not specifically* granted to the federal government in the Constitution belonged to the states and the people:

> The powers not delegated to the United States by the Constitution, nor prohibited by it to the States, are reserved to the States respectively, or to the people.

The federal government has no authority to assume additional powers unless the states and the people amend the Constitution to provide it additional powers. When the federal government tries to assume new powers on its own outside of its constitutional boundaries, the states and the people have the authority and the duty to rein it back in.

What Are Rights?

WE REALLY CAN'T continue a discussion about the structure of our government without first getting into a definition of rights.

The first thing we have to understand is that the Constitution doesn't *give* us our rights; it *guarantees* them. And the government doesn't give us our rights either; it *protects* them from foreign enemies and domestic criminals who threaten them. Instead, our rights come from God—we are born with them. As the Declaration of Independence states, we are *endowed* by our Creator with certain unalienable rights, including life, liberty, and the pursuit of happiness.

These "natural rights" are unalienable and universal for all human beings. Founding Father Thomas Paine in *Rights of Man* (1791) explained that natural rights could not be granted to the people by any charter or government, because that would mean they could also be taken away.

You are born naturally free, and as long as you do no harm to others or to society itself, no one can deprive you of that freedom. All other rights flow from these most basic rights of life and liberty, such as the right to own property, to speak freely, to freely associate with others, to practice the religion of your choosing, to bear arms, to be secure in your possessions, and to be free from unreasonable searches and seizures, among many others.

Moreover, when the Declaration of Independence states that all men are created equal, it is stating that the United States has no ruling class and that no one is born to be ruled by another. In America, all citizens are born equally free and independent. While we elect some people from among our ranks to be our leaders, they are not permanent rulers, we can fire them, and they still have to follow the law just like everyone else.

In addition, a constitution, a bill of rights, and a set of laws also ensure that your rights can't be voted away simply because a majority of the American people or their representatives in Congress don't like you. If the United States were simply based on majority rule, it could lead to an eventual "tyranny of the majority," which is something that our founding documents protect against.

The framers of the Constitution also knew that there would be people who would inevitably abuse their freedom by harming others and their property. Law enforcement officers and the courts exist to help catch and punish those who commit such wrongs. But the framers took great care to ensure that the government didn't unduly restrict the freedom of everyone just so the small percentage of bad actors and criminals would be prevented from harming others. For example, just because some people have the potential to abuse their free speech rights by illegally slandering others, doesn't mean the government reviews and censors every newspaper before it's printed. That's what a police state does; that's not how a free society operates.

What Rights Are Not

BIG-GOVERNMENT ADVOCATES—or statists—have argued from time to time that the clause in the Constitution that states "The Congress shall have Power To . . . provide for the common Defence and *general Welfare* of the United States" [emphasis added] means that the federal government is supposed to constantly improvise and grow to solve virtually any problem society encounters. Believers in an unlimited federal government seek to create an ever-expanding welfare state to redistribute wealth from the haves to the have-nots, and to take care of everyone by creating a cradle-to-grave "nanny state." Many politicians have used this General Welfare Clause as an excuse to grow government, and thus their own power and influence in the process.

Actually, "general welfare" means the general well-being of the country, not welfare to individuals. In both places it's mentioned in the Constitution, it's part of a clause about the government also providing for the common defense of the country. Thomas Jefferson explained that this wasn't some broad power to mother everyone:

> Congress has not unlimited powers to provide for the general welfare, but only those specifically enumerated [in the Constitution].

And James Madison echoed that same understanding:

> With respect to the words "General welfare" I have always regarded them as qualified by the detail of powers connected with them. To take them in a literal and unlimited sense, would be a metamorphosis of the Constitution into a character, which there is a host of proofs was not contemplated by its Creators.

To the extent that big-government statists even care about the Declaration of Independence anymore, they have also twisted the part of the Declaration identifying our right to "the pursuit of Happiness" to mean that happiness must be virtually *guaranteed* by government.

No, in fact, this turns the founding principles on their head. "The pursuit of Happiness" simply means because we have liberty, we have the *opportunity* to pursue happiness; we are not *guaranteed* happiness.

The statists also take the Declaration's statement that we are all "created equal" to mean that it's government's responsibility to ensure equal *results* for everyone.

The fact is that, in our founding tradition, "All men are created equal" means that no one is born to rule over another, that all citizens are treated equally under the law, and that our society has a goal of equal opportunity, not that everyone gets to have the same possessions, the same standard of living, or the same wage by government fiat. Government can only create a society of sameness by holding down some while propping up others. While those who are propped up may enjoy the free ride, those who are held down are held down against their will. That's oppression, not liberty.

Finally, statists also conclude that if the government doesn't provide the means for you to exercise a right, it hasn't done its job of *guaranteeing* that right. For example, in the debate over the federal health care law, we heard many discussions of people's "right" to health care. Unfortunately, people confused having the *freedom to exercise a right*—having the freedom to seek out, pay for, and receive legal health care without government interference—with forcing fellow citizens to pay for their health care so they could get it for free or at a reduced cost.

That's like saying that because you have a right to free speech, the government—with taxpayer money—must build you a podium and a microphone so you can exercise that right.

In the simplest form, you have a right—you have the freedom—to do most things and to obtain most things without *interference* from government or other citizens, but you don't have the "right" to demand other citizens (through government) give up what they have to help you. So-called rights that create an obligation for others to use their labor and their possessions to provide them for you are no rights at all. A right is an exercise of a freedom; it's not a claim to take someone else's freedom by forcing them into service for you.

I'll illustrate this point with an example the great free-market economist Walter E. Williams of Virginia's George Mason University has allowed me to share with you:

> Suppose I saw an elderly woman painfully huddled on a heating grate in the dead of winter. She's hungry and in need of shelter and medical attention. To help the woman, I walk up to you using intimidation and threats and demand that you give me $200. Having taken your money, I then purchase food, shelter, and medical assistance for the woman. Would I be guilty of a crime? A moral person would answer in the affirmative. I've committed theft by taking the property of one person to give to another.
>
> Most Americans would agree that it would be theft regardless of what I did with the money. Now comes the hard part. Would it still be theft if I were able to get three people to agree that I should take your money? What if I got 100 people to agree—100,000 or 200 million people? What if instead of personally taking your money to assist the woman, I got together with other Americans and asked Congress to use Internal Revenue Service agents to take your money?
>
> In other words, does an act that's clearly immoral and illegal when done privately become moral when it is done legally and collectively? The moral question is whether it's right to take what belongs to one person to give to another to whom it does not belong.
>
> Don't get me wrong. I personally believe that assisting one's fellow man in need by reaching into one's own pockets is praiseworthy and laudable. Doing the same by reaching into another's pockets is despicable, dishonest, and worthy of condemnation.

One clear illustration of the misconception about rights came during the debate over the Obamacare mandate that all employer health plans cover sterilization services, contraception, and abortifacients (drugs that induce abortions). I'll call it the "sterilization mandate." The sterilization mandate became extremely contentious for the Catholic Church, Catholic hospitals and schools, other churches, and certain business owners that provided employer-based health insurance for their employees. Under the government's sterilization mandate, religious institutions that had moral objections to sterilization, contraception, and abortifacients were nonetheless required to include these services in their employee health plans.

When these institutions objected and declared they wouldn't cover these services for their employees for reasons of conscience and religious liberty, political commentators railed on them, claiming that if contraceptives weren't covered in their health plans, policyholders would be denied their "right to contraception." Liberal commentators equated having a right to access contraceptives with having a "right" to *force* objecting employers to pay for them.

The fact was, no one was being denied access to contraceptives. No right was being violated. Even though churches refused to pay for coverage, employees were still free to go to their local pharmacies and purchase all the contraceptives they wanted. If there was any "right" in this situation at all, it was simply a right to *buy* contraceptives and *use* them without government interference. There was no right to have other citizens or employers pay to provide them.

All that said, although you have no "right" to things such as health care or welfare or a job, no one wants people who can't afford food to starve, no one wants people who can't afford health care to suffer, and no one wants people who can't afford housing to live on the streets. That's why most Americans believe in some form of safety net for those who truly cannot help themselves. I'll get into the safety net issue in chapter 3.

President Obama and a Constitution
of "Negative Liberties"

NOT SURPRISINGLY, PRESIDENT Obama had the polar opposite position about rights as I defined them above.

In a 2001 public radio interview, then–Illinois state senator Barack Obama said that the Constitution was too restrictive and didn't allow for the redistribution of wealth that he felt was needed in America. He pointed to what he thought was a failure of the U.S. Supreme Court under Chief Justice Earl Warren in its rulings on civil rights issues in the 1960s. In the interview, he said:

> [T]he Supreme Court never ventured into the issues of redistribution of wealth, and of more basic issues such as political and economic justice in society. . . . [The Supreme Court] didn't break free from the essential constraints that were placed by the Founding Fathers in the Constitution, at least as it's been interpreted, and the Warren Court interpreted in the same way, that generally the Constitution is a charter of negative liberties. Says what the states can't do to you. Says what the federal government can't do to you, but doesn't say what the federal government or state government must do on your behalf.
>
> And that hasn't shifted and one of the, I think, tragedies of the civil rights movement was because the civil rights movement became so court-focused I think there was a tendency to lose track of the political and community organizing and activities on the ground that are able to put together the actual coalition of powers through which you bring about redistributive change.

These remarks were echoed in Mr. Obama's statement to a voter caught on camera during the 2008 presidential campaign: "When you spread the wealth around, it's a good thing for everybody."

Barack Obama complained that the Constitution was a "charter of negative liberties" because it *limited* the power of the federal government rather than granted him unlimited power as president to take from the producers to fund the policy goals he had in mind for America.

During his presidency, we've seen Mr. Obama's many attempts to skirt the law and get around the Constitution to implement his redistributionist agenda. His crowning achievement was one of the most immense pieces of redistributionist legislation in American history—the federal health care law. With it, he effectively purchased his vision of Utopia at the expense of American liberty and the future of the American economy.

CHAPTER 3

SUBJECTS OR CITIZENS?

||||||||||||||||||||||||||||||||||||||||||||||||||||||||||||||||||||||||||||||||||||||||||||||||||||||||||||

Good intentions will always be pleaded for every assumption of
authority. It is hardly too strong to say that the Constitution was made
to guard the people against the dangers of good intentions. There are
men in all ages who mean to govern well, but they mean to govern.
They promise to be good masters, but they mean to be masters.

—DANIEL WEBSTER, famed orator and nineteenth-
century U.S. senator and secretary of state

LET ME TAKE you back to shortly before the American Revolution.
By 1775, hostilities had been growing for years between Great
Britain and its American colonies over taxes, punitive laws, and a lack
of colonial representation in Parliament.

The tensions only escalated as King George III and the British
Parliament determined they would make the Americans pay for British troops stationed in the colonies. Britain could have simply asked
the local representative legislatures in the colonies to tax the people to
contribute to their own defense, but Parliament insisted that it had the
authority to tax them directly. This only angered the colonists, who, in
turn, claimed their right as Englishmen not to be taxed without their
consent. They were rebuffed, however.

While Englishmen in Great Britain had elected members of Parliament to represent their interests, the Englishmen living in America—
who were still British subjects and were required to live under British

laws—had none. By refusing to allow the colonists a voice in national government, Parliament rarely had to consider their interests when imposing regulations and taxes on them.

The American colonists protested their second-class-citizen status, and a growing sense of rebellion ensued. And when they appealed to the king for relief, he turned a deaf ear. To stifle a wholesale uprising, King George III deployed standing armies to the colonies, forced colonists to feed and house troops in their homes, closed American ports of trade, and even had his royal colonial governors accuse the most troublesome Americans of fabricated crimes. To compound the injury, he then had the governors deprive the accused of trial by jury. The king also gave British officials open-ended search warrants, which allowed them to enter homes, warehouses, and ships to search them without cause. His governors abolished the locally elected legislatures, and the king and Parliament ruled the colonies from three thousand miles away.

The American revolution that would soon begin wasn't merely about "taxation without representation"; it was about the escalating violations of the colonists' core liberties.

Richmond, Virginia, March 23, 1775. Patrick Henry, George Washington, Thomas Jefferson, and other early American patriots from Virginia met at Henrico Parish Church (today, it's called St. John's Episcopal Church) to discuss the previous business of the First Continental Congress, their petitions of grievances to the king, and a plan for the defense of the colony should the tensions with Britain ultimately lead to war.

While several argued for a patient approach to see if Britain's ongoing disregard for their liberties would improve, Patrick Henry, a longtime and vocal defender of the rights of colonists and a representative in the House of Burgesses (the legislative body of the Virginia Colony), argued that they had long ago passed that point, and he advocated for resistance to the king's tyranny. He felt that the longer the colonists tolerated the abuses of their rights, the fewer rights they would eventually have. "Shall we acquire the means of effectual resistance, by lying supinely on our backs, and hugging the delusive phantom of hope, until our enemies shall have bound us hand and foot?" he asked his fellow delegates.

Of course, Henry's words were considered an act of treason by the Crown—an act for which he could be put to death. But his fervor to convince his fellow colonists to prepare to rise up against the king in the name of freedom went undeterred: "Should I keep back my opinions at such a time, through fear of giving offence, I should consider myself as guilty of treason towards my country, and of an act of disloyalty toward the majesty of heaven, which I revere above all earthly kings."

Henry, like many in the era of Enlightenment, believed that God created man to be free and that to take away that gift of freedom, as Great Britain had done, was a grievous offense toward the Creator.

Henry roused his fellow Virginians to prepare the colony for eventual war as he ended his speech with these now famous words, proclaiming he would rather die fighting for freedom than live as a slave under a tyrant: "Is life so dear, or peace so sweet, as to be purchased at the price of chains and slavery? Forbid it, Almighty God! I know not what course others may take; but as for me, give me liberty or give me death!"

Moved by his impassioned oration, the Colony of Virginia would begin to raise a militia to throw off the tyrannical chains of King George III and declare independence from Great Britain. And they would do it against seemingly insurmountable odds, because they would soon find themselves severely outnumbered, outfinanced, and outgunned.

Richmond, Virginia, March 23, 2010. After months of legislative maneuvers in Congress and public protests across America to attempt to stop the health care reform bill's passage, President Barack Obama signed the Patient Protection and Affordable Care Act—also known as the federal health care act, or Obamacare—into law. The new law, which would force every American to buy government-approved health insurance or face a penalty, was passed against the will of the majority of Americans and—I argued—in violation of the United States Constitution. Within an hour of the bill's signing, two of my senior attorneys walked to the federal courthouse in Richmond to file a lawsuit on behalf of the Commonwealth of Virginia to challenge the constitutionality of the unprecedented health insurance mandate.

It was not until later that evening—after the suit was filed, the calls of the day had been made, and all the media interviews were finished—that I realized that day, March 23, 2010, was the 235th anniversary *to the day* of Patrick Henry's "Give me liberty or give me death" speech . . . which he gave in Richmond, Virginia . . . just one mile away down the very same street from the federal courthouse where we filed suit.

I sat back for a moment and contemplated the historical connection of that day. On that anniversary, we began our fight for liberty against an unconstitutional federal mandate that could forever change the balance of power between the people and their government—one of the greatest threats to our liberty since our country's founding.

I went to my computer and looked up Henry's famous speech. These words struck me most:

> There is no longer any room for hope. If we wish to be free, if we mean to preserve inviolate those inestimable privileges for which we have been so long contending, if we mean not basely to abandon the noble struggle in which we have been so long engaged, and which we have pledged ourselves never to abandon, . . . we must fight!

Yes, I thought, we must fight . . . we must fight to preserve the very freedom that millions of American service men and women and other patriots throughout the course of America's previous 235 years sacrificed their lives and their fortunes to preserve for themselves and for future generations. I was just thankful to God that this time we fought with arguments in the courtrooms of America, and not with bullets on the bloody battlefields of war.

HOW DID WE ever get to this point where an American president and Congress were forcing citizens to buy health insurance, and where the states were suing the federal government to attempt to stop them?

Well, President Obama had campaigned on health care reform as a way to reduce health care costs and cover the nation's uninsured population. The plan was to create universal access to health care by mandating that the uninsured and everyone else obtain coverage by individually purchasing their own insurance, getting it through employer-offered health plans, participating in a new Medicaid (welfare) expansion that had lower eligibility requirements to let more people in, or buying it individually from a government-run "marketplace" of subsidized and heavily regulated health plans offered through health insurance exchanges that each state would create. Federal subsidies would be available to people based on financial need to offset the cost of the plans on the state exchanges.

The legislation to create all this started in the U.S. House of Representatives. In November 2009, the House passed the Affordable Health Care for America Act and then forwarded it to the U.S. Senate for consideration.

The House bill was more aggressive than many senators liked, so the Senate came up with its own bill, the Patient Protection and

Affordable Care Act (PPACA). Since the Constitution requires that all revenue-related bills originate in the House, senators took an unrelated House bill that was awaiting Senate consideration (it dealt with tax breaks for members of the military), gutted it of its original content, then used it as the vehicle—basically as a shell—for its version of a health care reform bill.

The Senate PPACA bill—which would ultimately become the health care bill that was passed into law—was built on the deception of the American people and paybacks to political allies. Because passing a massive tax on virtually all Americans to fund such a health care scheme would prove unpopular with the American people, the president and his allies in Congress decided that rather than create a health insurance *tax* to pay for coverage for the uninsured who couldn't afford insurance, they would instead create a *mandate* that would force all Americans to have health insurance or face a penalty. Indeed, few politicians wanted to be on record as raising taxes on Americans, especially during a deep recession.

The proponents insisted—right up to President Obama—that the mandate penalty was not a tax . . . at least that's what they said while they were trying to pass the bill . . .

PPACA's mandate required all people living in America who didn't have their own health insurance or who weren't covered by their employers or existing government programs to purchase government-approved health insurance for themselves and their dependents as of January 1, 2014, or be subject to a penalty of up to $695 per uninsured individual.

To obtain the required sixty-vote supermajority needed to overcome a certain Republican filibuster against the bill in the Senate, Democrat Senate majority leader Harry Reid offered "financial incentives" to some states to get their fence-sitting senators on board. Two particular paybacks were famously known as the "Cornhusker Kickback," for Nebraska Democrat senator Ben Nelson's vote, and the

"Louisiana Purchase" for Louisiana Democrat senator Mary Landrieu's vote. The paybacks included promises of significant increased federal funding for their Medicaid programs that would be paid for by taxpayer dollars from the other states. Shockingly, one arrangement permanently exempted Nebraska from paying its share of the billions in new increased Medicaid costs mandated by the health care bill (this shameless "incentive" was ultimately dropped).

These deals were effectively bribes, and the only place they were legal was in government.

Despite President Obama's promises of unmatched transparency and ethics that he claimed to have brought to Washington, the paybacks and deception were only the beginning. The health care "reform" bills were drafted mostly behind closed doors, and the Senate bill (the one that ultimately became the law) passed a Democrat-led Senate without even a committee hearing or report on Christmas Eve 2009, when most Americans were with family and friends, too busy to pay attention or to protest to stop it.

The week prior to its Senate passage, Republican senator from Kentucky Mitch McConnell angrily protested all the secrecy and the rush to pass a bill when no one was paying attention:

> Americans were told the purpose of reform was to reduce the cost of health care. Instead, Democratic leaders produced a $2.5 trillion, 2,074-page monstrosity that vastly expands government, raises taxes, raises premiums, and wrecks Medicare. And they want to rush this bill through by Christmas? They want to rush this bill through by Christmas that does all of these destructive things. One of the most significant, far-reaching pieces of legislation in U.S. history, and they want to rush it.
>
> Here is the most outrageous part. At the end of this rush, they want us to vote on a bill that no one outside

the majority leader's conference room has seen yet. No one has seen it. That is right. The final bill we vote on is not even the one we have had on the floor of the Senate. It is the deal Democratic leaders have been trying to work out in private. That is what they intend to bring to the Senate floor and force a vote on before Christmas. . . .

The only conceivable justification for rushing this bill is the overwhelming—overwhelming—opposition of the American people. Democrats know the longer Americans see this bill, the less they like it.

The PPACA bill that was rushed through the Senate was by no means complete, and several parts needed to be corrected. It wasn't drafted to be in its final form; it was drafted to get the 60 votes needed to get out of the Senate. Ultimately, the Senate leadership intended it to be amended by a conference committee of carefully selected House and Senate members and reconciled into a compromise bill, and the final version would have to be voted on again and get 60 votes in the Senate to pass.

But a fly in the ointment would soon emerge. Massachusetts Democrat senator Ted Kennedy had died back in the summer. A month later, Massachusetts governor Deval Patrick appointed former Democratic National Committee chairman Paul Kirk to fill Kennedy's vacant seat until a new senator could be elected in January 2010. Kirk was appointed to assure Democrats their 60-vote Christmas Eve supermajority.

The Democrats were confident that whoever replaced Kirk would also be a Democrat, because Massachusetts hadn't elected a Republican to the U.S. Senate since the 1970s. However, on January 19, 2010, to the surprise of many and in an act of defiance that seemed to indicate that even a liberal-leaning state like Massachusetts didn't want federal health care, Scott Brown, a Republican state senator who campaigned for the U.S. Senate on being the forty-first Republican vote needed to sustain a filibuster, defeated Massachusetts attorney general Martha Coakley to serve the balance of Kennedy's term. And that changed everything . . .

Now that Scott Brown had tipped the balance in the Senate, there were no longer sixty senators to stop a Republican filibuster. Any compromise bill created in a House/Senate conference committee or any amendments to the Senate bill in the House would have required 60 votes again in the Senate to pass. Since the Senate no longer had the 60 votes for the bill, the House would have to pass the Senate bill as it was.

O N THAT CHRISTMAS Eve of 2009 when the U.S. Senate passed its version of the health care bill—after I was elected, but before I was sworn in as Virginia's attorney general—Florida's then–attorney general Bill McCollum organized a conference call for several Republican state attorneys general to discuss what they would do if the bill passed the full Congress and became law. That call got the networking and discussions going among the states, which ultimately led to two of the three state lawsuits against Obamacare.

Once the bill passed the Senate with the individual-insurance mandate, I began to take a hard look at suing the government over the constitutionality of the mandate if it were ultimately enacted. I had consulted with the members of my transition team, as well as three attorneys who would become my deputies in the new attorney general's office—Wes Russell, Rick Neel, and David Johnson. I had also consulted my solicitor general, Duncan Getchell, a constitutional law expert who would take the lead in arguing our case in the courts.

As the bill moved through Congress from December through March, we monitored its progress. At the same time, several versions of a Virginia bill began making their way through Virginia's General Assembly. They were all referred to as the "Virginia Health Care

Freedom Act" (HCFA), and passing an HCFA was the top priority of the local Tea Party organizations during the 2010 session of the Virginia General Assembly. The HCFA basically said that no Virginian could be forced to buy health insurance against his or her will. The bills passed on a broad bipartisan basis.

Once passage of the federal bill began to appear imminent in mid-March, Duncan Getchell, Wes Russell, my senior appellate counsel Steve McCullough, and I began to draft Virginia's formal complaint and to finalize our constitutional reasoning for challenging the new law.

On Sunday, March 21, 2010, the U.S. House of Representatives passed the Senate's version of the health care bill, 219–212, without a single Republican vote. When I said earlier that health care reform was drafted behind closed doors, all one needs to remember is what Democrat Speaker of the House Nancy Pelosi said about the legislation: "But we have to pass the bill so that you can find out what is in it."

Even more depressing than that admission, it was evident that no member of Congress who had voted for the bill had actually bothered to read it.

The law was sold to the American people as a way to cover those who couldn't afford health insurance, and the most popular features were front-loaded and came into effect immediately in an effort to garner public support for the legislation. The first popular feature included letting full-grown adults stay on their parents' insurance until they reached age twenty-six (the supporters of Obamacare still called them "children" at this age, playing the infamous "but it's for the children" card that so often trumps reason and personal responsibility). The second popular feature prohibited insurance companies from denying coverage because of applicants' preexisting conditions. Although this aspect of the law was very popular, it was one of the fastest ways to put private insurance companies out of business, as the costs of treating these conditions could easily exceed the premiums companies would be allowed to charge policyholders with the conditions.

And the crafty politicians made sure the tab for all of it came later: the thousands of pages of regulations and restrictions that would have to be written by unelected bureaucrats to actually implement the law wouldn't come into effect until months or years after the law was passed, and the mandate to buy health insurance wouldn't come into effect until 2014.

A March 22 Reuters article summed up the widespread unpopularity and legal challenges the new law would soon face:

> Less than 24 hours after the House of Representatives gave final approval to a sweeping overhaul of healthcare, attorneys general from several states on Monday said they will sue to block the plan on constitutional grounds. Republican attorneys general in 11 states warned that lawsuits will be filed to stop the federal government overstepping its constitutional powers and usurping states' sovereignty. . . .
>
> In addition to the pending lawsuits, bills and resolutions have been introduced in at least 36 state legislatures seeking to limit or oppose various aspects of the reform plan through laws or state constitutional amendments, according to the National Conference of State Legislatures.

Despite the opposition from the American people and the states, President Barack Obama signed the Patient Protection and Affordable Care Act into law on March 23. Within the hour, we filed suit at the federal courthouse in Richmond.

The moment the lawsuit left my hands, I thought to myself, "If the federal government prevails, the Constitution and the whole foundation for the freest nation history has ever known will be gutted."

Our Congress and our president didn't seem to care that the law was widely unpopular or that the individual mandate might well be unconstitutional. They didn't care because their ultimate goal wasn't really about improving health care; it was about concentrating power over one-sixth of the national economy in the hands of the federal government, and therefore, to themselves.

The Policy Consequences of PPACA

ALTHOUGH MANY OF the debates leading up to the health care act's passage focused mostly on whether the law would reduce health care choices, increase health insurance costs, and create rationing, as an attorney general charged with upholding the law, I had to look at the act solely from a legal perspective. I thought the law was terrible policy, but once the law was passed, the policy battle was one we could not fight. In court, our job was to focus only on what was constitutional and what was not. Thus we targeted the health care law's individual-insurance mandate.

For that reason, I won't be getting into much of the policy of PPACA in this book. However, to remind you how bad this law is for the American health care system, I'll briefly mention some of its more controversial aspects.

First, the massive jump in regulatory requirements resulted in most insurance premiums actually going up, even though the president promised that the law would bring premiums down. Second, the law is costly at the federal level. The nonpartisan Congressional Budget Office issued a report in March 2012 estimating that the law would cost the American people $1.76 trillion between 2012 and 2022.

Third, the law is also costly at the state level, encouraging the states to expand their already costly Medicaid welfare programs to allow more low-income people who can't afford health insurance to get into those programs.

Fourth, the law is unbelievably costly for the private sector, requiring companies with more than fifty employees to provide an "affordable" employee health insurance plan or face an annual tax of $2,000 or $3,000 per employee. While this new tax will crush smaller companies that don't already have health plans, it will have the opposite effect on larger employers. Larger employers often have more generous health plans and pay significant portions of their employees' premiums. For them, paying the annual tax will likely be a cheaper option than paying the annual premium, so it would make sense for many to shut down corporate health plans and just pay the tax, leaving employees uninsured.

That reality led the Congressional Budget Office to issue a second report in March 2012, estimating that as many as 20 million people would lose their employer-based health insurance, leaving 26 to 27 million people still uninsured by 2022 (remember, we were told that PPACA would cover *all* of America's uninsured, not create new uninsured citizens).

Surveys also showed that because of the increased government interference in health care and greater cost controls imposed on doctors and their practices, many doctors would retire early, and aspiring doctors wouldn't even get into the profession, creating physician shortages and longer waits for care.

So much for achieving the stated objectives of the health care law: lowering costs and improving access for more people!

As a result of these consequences, many on both sides of the issue saw Obamacare as a first step to intentionally collapsing the private health insurance industry and the private health care system, so that a government takeover into a single-payer system would soon be inevitable. Before he became president, even Mr. Obama openly talked about the need to take incremental steps to ultimately get to a fully government-run health care system.

And there will surely be many more negative consequences yet to come. As of February 2012, the regulations created to implement the law were three times longer than the King James Version of the Bible—and the federal Department of Health and Human Services wasn't even finished writing them. There were still thousands more pages of rules to issue under the enormously lengthy law. More rules, more mandates, more hidden costs and fees, and more lost liberty.

Why Was More Government Needed to "Fix" Health Care When Government Was One of the Biggest Creators of the Problem?

I CAN CONFIDENTLY SAY that most of the attorneys general and governors fighting against the federal health care act agreed that significant parts of the U.S. health care system definitely needed fixing. We agreed that expenses were out of control and that not everyone's medical needs were being met. But we also agreed that giving up our very freedom for a system that allowed the government to further meddle in our private lives, control more of our economy, and bankrupt future generations to pay for its "solution" was not the answer.

And as an attorney general who swore an oath to uphold the law and the Constitution, I could never endorse a plan where government took away the rights of *all* so that it could provide a benefit—in this case, "affordable" health care—to some. While making health care coverage more affordable for all citizens was a laudable and worthy goal—a goal I pursued myself as a state senator—to concede our very freedom and the freedom of future generations to achieve that goal was a dangerous and inequitable exchange.

There were better solutions that Congress wouldn't even consider. One commonsense solution was to allow people to buy health insurance across state lines, which would increase competition, give consumers more choices, and necessarily lower prices. But most states had used a federal law from the 1940s to make buying health insurance across state lines *illegal*. Talk about killing competition!

There had also been proposals to allow consumers to shop around for their own insurance policies so they could choose the prices and coverages that best fit them. But the government flatly discourages that by only giving tax breaks to employers to buy health insurance policies; it refuses to give those same breaks to *individuals*— you know, actual people—which would effectively reduce the cost of premiums and put insurance coverage within the reach of more Americans.

There had been proposals to limit how much politicians could force insurers to cover certain conditions in their policies. Every time lawmakers mandated some new coverage or benefit to be included in even the most bare-bones policy, that meant higher premiums for everyone, which meant fewer families and businesses could afford the higher-cost policies.

More coverage mandates mean consumers are forced to pay for benefits they may never want or use because the insurance companies are required to offer them. Now, covering smoking cessation programs and tattoo removal may be great benefits for some policyholders, but why should I pay for smoking cessation and tattoo removal coverage every month if I've never smoked and I don't ever plan on getting a tattoo?

Imagine if you never ate kumquats or sweet potatoes, but the grocery store was required to include them in your grocery bag whenever you went shopping because some politician deemed them "necessary" staples for everyone. You weren't going to eat them, and they just spoiled month after month, but you had to pay for them with every grocery bill (because stores don't give them away for free). That's what happens with coverage mandates.

Mandated coverages, no tax breaks for individual insurance policies, and making the purchase of insurance across state lines illegal are just a few examples of some of the many factors that make health insurance more expensive. There are countless more. The point is, these are all a *direct result* of government meddling in the health insurance marketplace, thinking it knows what's best for everyone.

The problem with health insurance costs is not that there isn't enough government. It's that there's too much government!

Yet free-market solutions were stifled in the debate leading up to the passage of Obamacare. They were rejected out of hand, and not because they wouldn't work, but because they would take power away from Washington and put it back in the hands of the American people. The type of health care reform that empowered consumers over politicians just wasn't seriously considered. That was more evidence that Washington's goal was centralization and government control, not a better health care system.

The Government Is Not a Charity

ONE REASON THE American people got stuck with Obamacare was due to a devolution in American thinking over time that it was the government's job to provide health care for those who couldn't afford it on their own. But taking care of the poor is ideally the province first of families, churches, and charities, not the government.

In fact, public charity was never supposed to be a function of the federal government. James Madison, the "Father of the Constitution," in addressing the U.S. House of Representatives in 1794, said the federal government had no authority to use the people's treasury for charitable purposes:

> I cannot undertake to lay my finger on that article of the Constitution which granted a right to Congress of expending, on objects of benevolence, the money of their

constituents. . . . The government of the United States is a definite government, confined to specified objects. It is not like the state governments, whose powers are more general. Charity is no part of the legislative duty of the government.

I once heard a great illustration of why we shouldn't think of government as a charity: If you won $1 million in the lottery tomorrow and you wanted to use it to help the poor, would you donate it to a charity or give it to the government? Of course, most people would answer that they'd donate it to charity (I include churches under the general term charity in this section).

The next logical question is, Why? The answer is obvious: because you trust that the charity will get that money to people who really need the help *and* will accomplish that with minimal overhead cost. Most people don't have that same trust in government. In fact, a 2010 survey from the Center on Philanthropy at Indiana University showed that 94 percent of people polled said they trusted charities, while just 32 percent trusted Congress.

If that's the case—that most people would choose to give their money to charity over government—then why do we constantly turn to government to solve social problems instead of turning to our charities and churches, which we trust a whole lot more to get the job done, and done more efficiently?

Most charities have small professional staffs and rely heavily on volunteer help. This keeps their overhead costs significantly lower than large government social service bureaucracies. And lower overhead costs mean a larger proportion of every dollar gets to people in need.

Most charities also have local chapters run by local volunteer citizen boards and have more flexibility in dealing with clients and their varied situations, whereas federal programs often have to follow one-size-fits-all guidelines.

My coauthor, Brian Gottstein, experienced this type of government inflexibility when he worked for a well-known charity and got a phone call from a family in need of financial assistance to help pay for their son's medical bills. They called Brian when the caseworker at the government social services department told them they could get more financial help if the couple got a divorce. How utterly pathetic for a caseworker to suggest that a family break apart so they could be eligible for government assistance, when one of the few things that was giving them the strength to get through their difficult time was their love and support for one another.

Charities also have more incentive to stop those trying to defraud them: their funding is limited, and money taken by fraudsters is money that doesn't get to people in true need. On the other hand, as a state attorney general who runs my state's Medicaid Fraud Control Unit, I can tell you that estimates are that 10 percent of Medicaid dollars are stolen each year through fraud. As much as we work to stop it, the system is set up with so few checks on the front end that it's relatively easy to defraud the taxpayers for those who are determined to commit fraud. And unlike private charities, if the government's Medicaid program runs low on money, the government can just go back to the taxpayers to get more (or borrow more from the Chinese).

Private charities also have to prove that they're actually getting results with your money, or else people stop giving, and the charities shut down. Government never has to prove its programs are getting actual results. If there's waste, fraud, and abuse, or a program just isn't working, the agency and its taxpayer funding don't go away—the agency just gets "retooled," or gets even *more* funding, if anything is done at all. As Ronald Reagan once said, "A government bureau is the nearest thing to eternal life we'll ever see on this earth."

Finally, unlike charities, most government social service programs don't actually solve the underlying problem they're fighting. Despite spending trillions on federal welfare programs since President Lyndon

Johnson's War on Poverty began in 1964, poverty is—sadly—alive and well in America. According to the U.S. Census Bureau, the poverty rate in 1964 was 19 percent, and after the War on Poverty began, the rate has remained between 11 and 15.2 percent ever since. That's not exactly a successful war, especially for all the money that has been spent on it.

How many more years of going down the same path do we need before we call this approach a failure? Long before 1964, Benjamin Franklin warned us of the folly of throwing excessive amounts of public money at poverty, but in nearly 250 years, some of us still haven't learned this lesson of history:

> I am for doing good to the poor, but I differ in opinion of the means. I think the best way of doing good to the poor, is not making them easy in poverty, but leading or driving them out of it. In my youth I travelled much, and I observed in different countries, that the more public provisions were made for the poor, the less they provided for themselves, and of course became poorer. And, on the contrary, the less was done for them, the more they did for themselves, and became richer.

Over the years, an important lesson we've learned is that government programs tend to keep people in perpetual dependency; whereas with most charities, the philosophy is one of giving those in need a hand up, not a handout. Additionally, the charitable assistance is usually temporary, and job counseling and other programs are offered to help recipients get out of the bad situation they're in.

Michael Tanner of the libertarian think tank Cato Institute is the author of *The Poverty of Welfare: Helping Others in Civil Society*. He found that in 2012, the federal government spent more than $668 billion on at least 126 different programs to fight poverty, a dollar amount which didn't include welfare spending by state and local governments (an additional $284 billion). He calculated that those amounts came to $20,610 for every poor person in America, or $61,830 annually for a family of three. For that price, we could just hand the cash over to the poor every year and get rid of the government programs, and they'd be doing better financially than many middle-class Americans.

If instead of spending all this money on social service programs, the government left all those dollars in the hands of the taxpayers, Americans would have more money to donate to private charities and churches, just as they did in the 1980s when Ronald Reagan simplified the tax structure and lowered tax rates.

Richard McKenzie, a professor at the Graduate School of Management at the University of California at Irvine, analyzed charitable giving during the 1980s and reported in a 1992 *National Review* article: "The annual rate of growth in total giving in the 1980s was nearly 55 per cent higher than in the previous 25 years." He said that no matter how the records of giving were measured, the 1980s was "in fact a decade of renewed charity and generosity."

So why does government social welfare continue to grow?

Often, it is simply because politicians want to be liked. When groups come to politicians asking them to create a new government program, increase funding for an existing one, send money to a poor foreign country, or keep extending unemployment benefits into a period of years, politicians often do so because they don't want to be labeled "selfish" (that's bad for reelection) and, frankly, because the money doesn't come out of their own pockets. But it's not selfish to be frugal with money that belongs to someone else, and it's certainly not compassion when you're giving away other people's money.

Compassion for the poor shouldn't be defined by how much politicians fund welfare programs so they can buy more reelection votes with the taxpayers' money. Compassion should be defined by the assurance that the largest percentage of every dollar meant for the poor goes to the poor, and that every dollar and every volunteer hour goes to trying to lift the poor person out of his situation and doesn't go to keeping him in perpetual dependency on government. After nearly fifty years of the War on Poverty, we should know by now that the most effective help and compassion come from private charity, not from the government.

Of course, when you're an attorney general fighting against "government-guaranteed health coverage for everyone," you get criticized in newspaper editorials, letters to the editor, and across the Internet for lacking compassion. But I can tell you from personal experience, I certainly understand the plight of those who don't have health insurance.

When I was a boy in the 1970s and my dad was changing jobs, my mother became very ill during a brief lapse in my family's health insurance. During her six months of hospitalization and medical treatment, it wasn't always clear she would survive. As we grappled with the thought of possibly losing her, medical bills drove our family deeper in debt. While my parents could have declared bankruptcy, they didn't.

When my mother finally returned home from the hospital, my younger brother didn't know who she was. He didn't remember her.

My parents did what most families did back then: they reached out to our extended family—we moved to the same street as my grandparents, so they could help care for my brother and me; friends helped with babysitting, trips to the doctor, and even meals; and my dad kept working to pay off the medical bills.

It was a painfully difficult time for my parents, and one I would wish on no one, but despite the hardship, the last thing my parents thought about doing was asking the government to force other people to pay our bills.

The lesson that life isn't necessarily fair and that it's not government's job to make it fair is worth learning early on in life. My own mother taught me that. She taught me that when things seemed unfair, complaining wasn't the answer; working harder was the answer.

I wasn't supposed to compare what I had against what others had; I was just supposed to work hard and make my life the best that I could. My parents and my faith also taught me that in the process, I was supposed to voluntarily help others; and by helping others, my own life would be enriched.

My wife, Teiro, keeps me grounded in the real-world implications of my job as an elected official, just as she did during the health care lawsuit. She was the first person to point out that if Virginia won the lawsuit, when anyone had trouble paying for medical care, I would probably get blamed for it. They wouldn't care about the Constitution or the law; they'd just care about the fact that they couldn't afford their own medical care. And because of my parents' experience, I knew that was a very real fear for people.

Barack Obama understood that fear, too, and he manipulated it to his advantage in the health care reform battle. And he did so despite the fact that his "compassionate" solution contradicted his oath to the American people and to God to uphold the Constitution of the United States of America.

The Government Is Not Benevolent

WHY DID SO many people have so much faith that government could reduce health care costs when all its interventions in the past only seemed to make the situation worse? For forty-five years, we'd had one and only one solution to every health care concern: more government. As Dr. Phil would ask, "How's that working out for you?"

A popular definition of insanity is doing the same thing over and over and expecting a different result. Maybe it's time to try less government instead of more government.

Why had people been willing to place so much faith in an altruistic government they thought would do the "right thing" and look out for their best interests, when it's run by politicians who have their own personal motivations?

We treat government as if it has the guiding moral authority of a church and the benevolent heart of a charity. But it has neither, and we shouldn't expect it to. In my career, I've seen many outstanding elected leaders driven by a desire to serve the public; but unfortunately, I've seen too many others who are driven by their own self-interest, greed, or a desire to accumulate power. For the latter group, it's precisely the people's reliance on government that they count on . . . in fact, they prey on it.

Your government will never love you. It can't.

And your government is *forbidden* from nurturing your soul—the most important reservoir of personal strength.

Churches and charities *can* love you and nurture your soul. On its best days, government can never compete with churches or charities to deliver either faith or love—essential ingredients for any person to be complete.

Government is not inherently bad, but we always have to protect the country against bad people in government and good people in government acting badly. The Constitution was created because the founders knew from thousands of years of human history that power concentrated in the hands of a few inevitably led to the disappearance of basic human rights. Renowned economist Milton Friedman, in his book *Capitalism and Freedom*, stressed this very point:

> Our minds tell us, and history confirms, that the great threat to freedom is the concentration of power. Government is necessary to preserve our freedom, it is an instrument through which we can exercise our freedom; yet by concentrating power in political hands, it is also a threat to freedom. Even though the men who wield this power initially be of good will and even though they be

not corrupted by the power they exercise, the power will
both attract and form men of a different stamp.

The framers knew that our leaders would be human and fallible, and that no matter what age in history—whether 976 or 1776 or 2076—those leaders not bound by a set of laws would seek power at the cost of the people's liberty. They would succumb to personal ambition, prejudices, fear, and intimidation, or even a desire to do the will of those they represented, even if that will didn't comport with the Constitution or the law.

That's why the framers limited the power of those in government through the Constitution and the Bill of Rights, and by dividing government to ensure that no branch took too much control. Additionally, the framers made those in government ultimately accountable to the people. In other words, there was to be no blind faith in government or in the people who ran it.

James Madison stressed this point in *Federalist No. 10* when he wrote, "Enlightened statesmen will not always be at the helm." He also said in *Federalist No. 51* that "if men were angels, no government would be necessary." Well, we aren't angels. That's a point we reprove over and over.

Sometimes bad politicians set out to grow government in order to increase their own power and influence. This phenomenon doesn't just happen in Washington; it happens at all levels of government. The amazing thing is that they often grow government without protest from citizens, and sometimes they even get buy-in from citizens—at least from the ones getting the goodies.

One of their favorite ways to increase their power is by creating programs that dispense subsidized government benefits, such as Medicare, Social Security, and outright welfare (Medicaid, food stamps, subsidized housing, and the like). These programs make people dependent on government. And once people are dependent, they feel they can't afford to have the programs taken away, no matter how inefficient, poorly run, or costly to the rest of society.

We saw these fears played upon infamously in the 2012 presidential campaign in the "Mediscare" ads attacking the Republican ticket in which Granny gets shoved off a cliff in her wheelchair. It calls to mind H. L. Mencken's quote: "The whole aim of practical politics is to keep the populace alarmed (and thence clamorous to be led to safety) by menacing it with a whole series of hobgoblins."

The worst politician's intent is to get as many people dependent on getting a check or service from the government as possible, because the more people who are dependent on big government, the more people there are who will vote to keep or expand big government in the next election. Citizens will vote for those politicians who promise more benefits each year, rather than the fiscally responsible politicians who try to point out that such programs are unsustainable and will eventually bankrupt the states or the nation.

Creating government dependency is the typical method of operation for big-government statists. But sometimes even small-government conservatives can stray from their principles and fall into this way of legislating. They often succumb to reelection pressures or to the constant portrayals by some in the media and big-government advocacy groups as being "mean" and "heartless" by not using "their power" to help others.

We don't have to go far to find examples of conservatives going astray. One such example was the creation of a subsidized prescription drug program for senior citizens called Medicare Part D. It was the largest entitlement program in forty years, and it was created under Republican president George W. Bush and passed by a Republican-controlled House and a Republican-controlled Senate in 2003. While there may have been some good intentions involved, this was George W. Bush using taxpayer dollars to buy seniors' votes for his 2004 reelection campaign, pure and simple. And the Republicans in Congress generally went right along with it.

Republicans also grew the government with programs like No Child Left Behind—an expensive public education initiative that also increased the federal government's tentacles into an area that is most appropriately within the purview of the states. Then there was the Troubled Asset Relief Program (TARP), a program that spent hundreds of billions of dollars to bail out financial institutions from bad mortgage loans they made to people who couldn't pay them back. I'm not afraid to say that I was embarrassed for my party over these votes. Because of these programs and others, the Republicans lost much of their own moral authority to criticize increased spending under President Obama and the Democrat-controlled Congress that would follow.

Whether you're liberal, conservative, libertarian, or politically agnostic, everyone should have a healthy skepticism and apprehension about big government, just as the founders did. We need to appreciate how much the Constitution and its Bill of Rights protect each of us from those in power who would use that power against us. I've been known—and sometimes shunned—throughout my political career for trying to hold Republicans to the principles of limited government as doggedly as I try to hold Democrats to them. I didn't write this book so much as a Republican, but as an American worried about the future of our country.

Thomas Jefferson warned us all the way back in 1798 that we should always be wary of the people we entrust with so much power:

> [C]onfidence is everywhere the parent of despotism; free government is founded in jealousy, and not in confidence; it is jealousy, and not confidence, which prescribes limited constitutions to bind down those whom we are obliged to trust with power; that our Constitution

has accordingly fixed the limits to which, and no farther, our confidence may go. . . . In questions of power, then, let no more be said of confidence in man, but bind him down from mischief by the chains of the Constitution.

Government's power was limited precisely because the framers knew the ability to use that power would occasionally attract the wrong leaders, whether they were evil or just weak. With the Constitution limiting politicians' authority to act, except for the most lawless ones, it would be hard for them to do permanent harm before being fired at the next election.

Unfortunately, President Obama didn't feel compelled by his oath of office to be bound by the Constitution or to federal laws. His disregard for both has caused incalculable long-term damage to American liberty and to the people's faith that their government still exists to protect it.

CHAPTER 4

COULD CONGRESS REALLY FORCE
AMERICANS TO BUY THINGS?

IIIIIIIIIIIIIIIIIIIIIIIIIIIIIIIIIIIIIIIIIIIIIIIIIIIIIIIIIIIIIIIIIIIIIIIIIIIIIIIIIIIIIIIIIIIIIIIIIIIIIIIIIIIIIIIIIIIIIIIII

> *When all government, domestic and foreign, in little as in*
> *great things, shall be drawn to Washington as the center of*
> *all power, it will render powerless the checks provided of*
> *one government on another and will become as venal and*
> *oppressive as the government from which we separated.*

> —THOMAS JEFFERSON on the concentration of power
> in Washington and away from the states, 1821

DURING HIS CAMPAIGN for president, Barack Obama told everyone how ill-conceived a health insurance mandate on the American people would be. In February 2008, then-candidate Obama appeared on the *Ellen DeGeneres Show*, where he denounced such a mandate proposed by his opponent for the presidential nomination, Hillary Clinton:

> She'd have the government force every individual to buy
> insurance, and I don't have such a mandate because I
> don't think the problem is that people don't want health
> insurance. It's that they can't afford it, . . . Well, if things
> were that easy, I could mandate everybody buy a house,
> and that, you know, and that would solve, you know, the
> problem of homelessness. It doesn't.

He was right. Unfortunately for the American people, he changed his mind, and the illogical mandate he denounced eventually became the centerpiece of his health care plan.

But why a mandate and not a tax? In the past, Congress used the income tax and other taxing powers—including tax credits, tax deductions, and other incentives—and its spending power as its authority to create social welfare programs like Social Security and Medicaid. Why didn't it just increase taxes to create this new program? The answer was that Congress lacked the political will to vote on taxes large enough to pay for its health care scheme. And remember, the president pledged during his campaign that under his administration, no one making less than $250,000 a year would face a tax increase.

So, lawmakers and the president tried an "end run" around the taxing power by using an unprecedented and expanded interpretation of the Commerce Clause of the Constitution, claiming that under Congress's power to regulate interstate commerce, it could force citizens *into* commerce to buy health insurance by charging them a *penalty* if they didn't. That way, no one could call it a tax increase (except, later, the administration *had* to call it a tax to avoid having PPACA struck down by the courts as unconstitutional. But I'll get to that twisted word game in the next chapter).

The problem was, however, in the 220-plus years since the Constitution was written, the federal government had *never* before used the power of the Constitution's Commerce Clause—the power "[t]o regulate Commerce with foreign Nations, and among the several States, and with the Indian tribes"—to *force* individuals to engage in commerce—to force them to buy a product or service from another private entity or face a penalty—as a condition of residence in the United States.

Before passing PPACA, the Senate even expressed doubt that it had the power to adopt the individual mandate. The Senate Finance Committee asked the Congressional Research Service to issue an opinion on the constitutionality of the mandate. The CRS replied:

"Whether such a requirement would be constitutional under the Commerce Clause is perhaps the most challenging question posed by such a proposal, as it is a novel issue whether Congress may use this Clause to require an individual to purchase a good or a service."

Despite the grave uncertainty, as well as the fact that the mandate would radically alter the balance of power between the government and the people, Congress still voted to foist the mandate on the American people.

As I noted in chapter 1, the principle that the federal government didn't have the power to order Americans to buy things goes all the way back to America's colonial period. Yet our government attempted to force free American *citizens* to do what the tyrant we rebelled against didn't have the authority to do when we were his *subjects*. The gall of our elected leaders was beyond all bounds.

In fact, I'd like to point out an interesting story on this issue of citizens versus subjects. In 2009, a preservation scientist at the Library of Congress used sophisticated computer-aided imaging to examine Thomas Jefferson's rough draft of the Declaration of Independence and discovered that Mr. Jefferson made an interesting word correction during his drafting of the document.

The author of the Declaration of Independence had originally written the phrase "our fellow subjects." But he apparently changed his mind about using that term for his fellow colonists, because scrawled over the word *subjects* instead was the word *citizens*.

As the Library of Congress put it, "The correction seems to illuminate an important moment for Jefferson and for a nation on the eve of breaking from monarchical rule: a moment when he reconsidered his choice of words and articulated the recognition that the people of the fledgling United States of America were no longer subjects of any nation, but citizens of an emerging democracy."

What makes the American experience in liberty so unique is the notion that the *citizens are sovereign*—that is, they are the ones who hold the ultimate power over government, and the government is subject to their will. Using the Commerce Clause to mandate that citizens buy health insurance turned that entire concept upside down, as government sought to force citizens to do *its* will.

The Commerce Clause

THE MEANING OF the word *commerce* in both the English language and in the law has been fairly consistent since the time of our founders. It has always meant trading, buying and selling, or transporting of goods, services, and tangible property. It meant that then; it means the same thing now. So, it wasn't as if the Commerce Clause was written in some ancient language that needed to be reinterpreted for modern times.

The framers of the Constitution originally intended the interstate part of the Commerce Clause (as opposed to the parts about commerce with foreign nations and Indian tribes) to prevent the states from imposing protectionist tariffs and other trade barriers against imports from other states. The framers were experiencing just that kind of commercial warfare under the Articles of Confederation, and it was killing their economies and threatening the unity of the states. In fact, fixing this very problem was the primary motivation for representatives of the states to gather first in Annapolis in 1786, and then, more famously, in Philadelphia in 1787.

James Madison explained the purpose of the "power to regulate commerce among the several States" in a letter in 1829:

> Yet it is very certain that it grew out of the abuse of the power by the importing States in taxing the non-importing, and was intended as a negative and preventive provision against injustice among the States themselves,

rather than as a power to be used for the positive purposes of the General Government, in which alone, however, the remedial power could be lodged. [Emphasis added.]

So the Commerce Clause was clearly intended to keep the channels of free trade open among the states. It was never meant to restrict commerce, nor was it intended as a catchall authority to give the federal government additional powers over all commercial activity among the states, and it certainly was never intended to be used to *force* citizens into commerce. In fact, the framers viewed government regulation of economic activity as illegitimate unless that activity harmed or threatened to harm someone else.

For the first hundred years of our national existence, the Commerce Clause functioned just as Madison and the framers had expected. However, beginning with the Interstate Commerce Act in 1887 and the Sherman Antitrust Act in 1890, Congress began asserting more affirmative power under the Commerce Clause.

In the 1930s and 1940s, the U.S. Supreme Court under President Franklin Roosevelt helped to expand the commerce powers of the federal government beyond what the framers could have ever imagined. In a 1942 ruling, *Wickard v. Filburn,* the court held that the Commerce Clause allowed Congress to regulate the amount of wheat a farmer grew on his own land for his family's and farm's consumption.

The Supreme Court in *Wickard* said that "even if [an] activity be local and though it may not be regarded as commerce, it may still, whatever its nature, be reached by Congress if it exerts a *substantial economic effect* on interstate commerce, and this irrespective of whether such effect is what might at some earlier time have been defined as 'direct' or 'indirect.'" Thus was born the "substantial effects" test, which—of course—has never been clearly defined. But, don't worry, government knows it when it sees it.

The court's logic in *Wickard* was that if enough other people did the same thing as Farmer Filburn—basically, rely on themselves for their wheat rather than going into the market and buying it—the aggregate effect would reduce the demand for the purchase of wheat, which would have a "substantial economic effect" on interstate wheat prices, because less demand leads to lower prices. Because Congress wanted to regulate wheat prices (to keep them high), the court said the government had an interest in regulating wheat production even when such wheat was not going to be sold into commerce!

Wickard v. Filburn was a terrible court ruling and the most expansive stretching of the Commerce Clause in American history. (Yet with the health insurance mandate, President Obama sought to go even further.) The court's *Wickard* decision allowed an enormous expansion of Congress's power over the economy.

Finally, in the 1980s, the court, under Chief Justice William Rehnquist, began to require the government to articulate some "limiting principle" to any new expansion of Congress's Commerce Clause authority. In other words, there had to be some identifiable limit to the power the government claimed, because if there wasn't one, the government could force the American people to do just about anything it wanted, which is not how a supposedly limited government works.

So as the lawsuits against the federal health care act worked their way through the courts, the lawyers for the Obama administration were repeatedly asked by federal judges to articulate some limiting principle to the insurance mandate. "If the government can force people to buy health insurance, what can't they force citizens to buy?" was a question repeated again and again, with no real answer ever given by the federal government. That was because no limiting principle existed.

The federal government tried to hang its mandate hat on the "substantial effects" test. It argued that if enough people did not buy health insurance, that decision would be an "activity" that would have a "substantial effect" on the health insurance and health care markets. The

71

administration argued that opting *not* to buy health insurance—doing nothing—affects commerce because uninsured people inevitably require health care, and when they don't have the money or insurance to pay for it, that raises costs for everyone else.

The government estimated that every American family with health insurance paid an average of $1,000 more a year in premiums to cover the care of those who didn't have insurance. It also claimed that it wasn't regulating inactivity—doing nothing—because "none of us is a bystander when it comes to health care. All of us need health care eventually," meaning that almost everyone would eventually be in the market to buy health insurance or health care—or, put another way, everyone would eventually enter the stream of commerce.

The first problem with this argument was that people who hadn't bought insurance weren't yet engaged in commerce, and the government was attempting to force them into it. "The government can't draft an unwilling citizen into commerce just so it can regulate him under the Commerce Clause," Virginia's solicitor general, Duncan Getchell, argued in court.

The second problem was the same reasoning could be used to claim that the government had the authority to force you to buy a car, because if you didn't buy a car, you were making an economic decision that would inevitably affect others because sometime in your life, you would have to use publicly subsidized transportation—a bus, a train, et cetera. And the government would not only have the authority to force you to buy a car, but could tell you what kind of car (GM, of course) and what features were required.

What about food? At some point, we all need food. Eventually, we all would be in the market to buy food—or as in the case of Farmer Filburn, we could grow our own food, which the courts might then determine had a regulable substantial effect on interstate commerce—so why couldn't the government mandate that we buy food, and even certain kinds of food? Perhaps broccoli or asparagus—the two most often mentioned by judges during the health care hearings.

What about shelter? At some point, we all need shelter. Why couldn't the government mandate that we buy houses? (This one sounds eerily familiar for some reason.)

The other problem with this reasoning was that because it was allowed to regulate only activity, the government tried to convince the courts that a *mental decision* to not buy health insurance was actually an *activity* that it could regulate. It said that being uninsured was "an economic decision," and that decision was an activity that had "a substantial effect on interstate commerce." The government was no longer just trying to regulate activity, but inactivity, as well. If it could regulate activity and inactivity, what would possibly be outside of its reach? How could the government penalize a citizen for just doing nothing?

This awkward reasoning was well outside of the established limits of the Commerce Clause. Frankly, it was well outside the established limits of common sense, to say nothing of the implications for liberty.

Virginia argued that being uninsured was a decision to do nothing, and that doing nothing—by definition—is not an activity. The Commerce Clause had *always* been used to regulate economic activity, never inactivity. And since the government could regulate only activity, it had no business forcing us to buy health insurance.

Regardless of what anyone thought of the goals of the health care law—making insurance more affordable for some people, covering the poor, et cetera—allowing the federal government this kind of raw power to attempt to reach those goals was a very dangerous precedent to set.

That wasn't rhetoric. That was reality.

Imagine how apoplectic the big-government statists would get if Congress voted to force everyone to buy a gun! Nancy Pelosi would have sung a different tune over that one. The power was the same, and the possibilities were virtually limitless as to what citizens could be forced to buy.

For the two years that the health care battle lasted, I challenged anyone who doubted this analogy to explain how the federal government could compel one purchase (health insurance) but not the other (a gun). To this day, no one has been able to logically explain that it couldn't. As I said before, even the federal government wasn't able to articulate a limit in court.

In fact, in 2010, I had a debate at the Washington Legal Foundation with someone I considered an expert on such matters: Walter Dellinger, former acting U.S. solicitor general under President Bill Clinton. When he was asked what remaining limit on federal power would there be if the federal health insurance mandate was deemed constitutional, Dellinger answered: political.

Political limits. What he meant by that was that the only limit to restrain federal power would be the will of the majority in Congress. Well, that's no restraint at all.

Why have a constitution that's supposed to restrain the power of the federal government if all you need is a majority vote in Congress to break those restraints and take away the people's liberty? That would be like—as the old saying goes—the fox guarding the henhouse.

But If Social Security and Medicare Aren't Unconstitutional, Why Is Obamacare?

How COULD THE health care law be unconstitutional if Social Security and Medicare are legal? And why can states mandate the purchase of auto insurance, but the federal government couldn't mandate the purchase of health insurance?

Well, as I said previously, Social Security is constitutional because the government uses its *constitutional* taxing authority to levy a tax on employment, and then it uses its *constitutional* spending authority to spend money on Social Security payments. Similarly, Medicare is a constitutional exercise of the government's taxing and spending powers.

The federal government did not, however, have a constitutional power to force citizens to buy private goods, especially when they weren't engaging in any activity.

To the second question about state-mandated auto insurance, the Constitution lays out specific and limited powers for the federal government, and, again, none of those powers is a power to mandate that citizens purchase private goods.

The Tenth Amendment to the U.S. Constitution states that all other powers not specifically delegated to the federal government in the Constitution are reserved "to the States respectively, or to the people." States are assumed to have virtually any power they need, except powers they're prohibited from exercising by their respective constitutions or by federal law. The states have many powers that the federal government does not. For example, the states *do* have the authority to impose health insurance mandates if they so choose. That's why the health insurance mandate Mitt Romney enacted in Massachusetts when he was governor was perfectly legal. The difference between Obamacare and Romneycare is that states are allowed to enact purchasing mandates; the federal government is not.

Additionally, buying auto insurance is something states can require as a condition of letting you drive on public roads. But you don't have to get car insurance if you're willing to forego driving. Buying health insurance under a federal mandate would not be voluntary, as you would be required to buy it simply because you were breathing.

In February 2011, I testified before the U.S. House Judiciary Committee about our court challenge to the health care law. The most interesting exchange of the day was with Democrat congressman Jerrold Nadler of New York.

In my exchange with the congressman, I explained my position that constitutionally, states *could* order their citizens to buy things—including health insurance—while the federal government could *not*. (Of course, Virginia and a few other states had passed laws saying that neither the federal nor the state government could mandate the purchase of health insurance, because we thought mandates were just bad policy. But absent a state law like that or a state constitutional provision forbidding it, states were not prohibited from ordering their citizens to buy things.)

I took the further position that this distinction between the powers of states and the federal government was an important protection for liberty. Finally, I reminded him that the health care case was not really about health care; it was about liberty.

Mr. Nadler took issue with my contention that the case was about liberty, and he had an interesting line of attack. He said that so long as *either* the federal government *or* the state governments could order the purchase of health insurance, then liberty couldn't be at stake because the only distinction was between one level of government or another. Six of one, a half dozen of the other. No difference.

Put differently, according to Congressman Nadler, if states could order you to buy health insurance just as he wanted to allow the federal government to do, then from the perspective of the citizen, there was absolutely no difference to your liberty. Was he right?

Absolutely not! Actually, he made two mistakes.

The first mistake was that he broke the world of government down incorrectly. He lumped state governments in with the federal government. If everyone was in a room together, the congressman saw the federal and state governments together on the left side of the room and the people on the right side.

But that wasn't how the founders broke it down. With the Tenth Amendment (the federal government only having certain specifically enumerated powers, with the rest left to the states or the people), the founders saw the federal government on the left side of the room and the state governments together with the people on the right.

And within each state, the people had decided how much power their own state government would have vis-à-vis the citizens of that particular state. The people of all fifty states had made different choices about the balance between themselves and their state governments. Those choices decided the balance between state (and local) government power and citizens' liberty on a state-by-state basis.

Of course, state and local governments can deny us our liberty, too; however, they are closer to the people and therefore more easily "fixed" when they go astray. As a last resort, if things are that bad, people can move to another state.

Thus, Nadler's first mistake led directly to his second: by lumping state and federal governments together, he forgot that the Constitution's firm separation of their spheres of authority put them in tension with one another in a way that was intended to allow each to check the other, thereby protecting the liberty of the people.

We call that "federalism," Congressman.

How Virginia Was Able to Sue the Federal Government

IN MARCH 2010, thanks in large part to the grassroots pressure put on state legislators by the Virginia Tea Party, Virginia became the first state in the nation to pass a law prohibiting government from requiring citizens to buy health insurance against their will. Governor Bob McDonnell and large bipartisan majorities in both houses of the General Assembly (90 to 3 in the House and 25 to 15 in the Democrat-controlled Senate) adopted Virginia's antimandate Health Care Freedom Act (HCFA) before President Obama signed Obamacare into law.

Therefore, when the president signed the federal health care bill, it came into direct conflict with Virginia's HCFA.

This conflict of laws gave Virginia the standing to sue. Under the Supremacy Clause of the Constitution, the federal law—if constitutional—would invalidate a Virginia law, which meant Virginia's ability to enforce its own laws had been "injured."

Since only one law could prevail, and since the attorney general of Virginia has a duty to defend all validly enacted state laws from any challenge, my office filed suit asking a federal court to determine which law should prevail. We asked the court to find that Congress had exceeded its authority by imposing the individual mandate. Such a ruling would allow the HCFA to stand.

Virginia filed its own lawsuit, while twelve other states joined Florida in filing a multistate suit* on the same day. While we fully supported the Florida lawsuit, the venue to defend a Virginia law was rightly a federal court in Virginia, not in Florida.

Many in Congress and in the media questioned whether states could even bring lawsuits against the federal government. From Reuters (March 26, 2010):

> While some legal scholars think the suits will reach the
> Supreme Court, many agree that the supremacy clause of
> the Constitution, which puts the powers of the U.S. gov-
> ernment above those of the states, will trump the states'
> arguments.

---

*The original thirteen plaintiffs in the multistate suit on March 23, 2010, were Florida, Alabama, Colorado, Idaho, Louisiana, Michigan, Nebraska, Pennsylvania, South Carolina, South Dakota, Texas, Utah, and Washington. It was a bipartisan effort that included Louisiana's Democrat attorney general. A total of twenty-six states were eventually part of the multistate suit that went to the United States Supreme Court. The additional states that joined the multistate suit were Alaska, Arizona, Georgia, Indiana, Iowa, Kansas, Maine, Mississippi, Nevada, North Dakota, Ohio, Wisconsin, and Wyoming. Virginia and Oklahoma filed their own lawsuits.

The Supremacy Clause of the Constitution states:

> This Constitution, and the Laws of the United States
> *which shall be made in Pursuance thereof*; and all Treaties
> made, or which shall be made, under the Authority of the
> United States, shall be the supreme Law of the Land;
> and the Judges in every State shall be bound thereby, any
> Thing in the Constitution or Laws of any State to the
> Contrary notwithstanding. [Emphasis added.]

Normally, conflicts of state and federal laws would be decided in favor of the federal government, but the wording of the Supremacy Clause expressly *limits* federal supremacy to laws that are made *in accordance* with the Constitution. If a federal law is deemed unconstitutional in federal court while a conflicting state law is constitutional, the state law should prevail.

Despite the surprise and indignation of many in Congress that states could actually challenge the laws they pass, as Supreme Court Justice Sandra Day O'Connor once noted, resolving such disputes has been one of the primary functions of the federal courts almost since the Constitution's inception:

> [T]he task of ascertaining the constitutional line between federal and state power has given rise to many of the Court's most difficult and celebrated cases. . . . [T]he Court has resolved questions "of great importance and delicacy" in determining whether particular sovereign powers have been granted by the Constitution to the Federal Government or have been retained by the States.

With our court challenges, Virginia and the other states weren't doing anything but following what the Constitution prescribed, and acting as a check in our system of checks and balances—just as the founders intended.

The Biggest Battle over the Mandate: Different Interpretations of the Constitution

On every question of construction carry ourselves back to the time when the Constitution was adopted, recollect the spirit manifested in the debates and instead of trying what meaning may be squeezed out of the text, or invented against it, conform to the probable one in which it was passed.

—THOMAS JEFFERSON, 1823

IN THE PUBLIC debate over the challenge to the federal health care law, a lot of the arguments centered on different interpretations of the Constitution's Commerce Clause power. Would the judges and justices who heard the cases continue to "reinterpret" the language of the Constitution to expand the Commerce Clause's reach, or would they finally see that there had to be limits to this already immense power the federal government used to regulate everything from a farmer's harvest for his personal consumption to virtually any product made or traded in America, even if it never crossed state lines?

The debate over how the words of the Constitution should be interpreted is one that has raged on since the day it was ratified. Small-government conservatives are often called "strict constructionists" when it comes to how they read the Constitution. They feel the only way to be consistent in the law is to read the words according to their original meaning at the time they were written . . . just as Thomas Jefferson called on us to do in 1823.

But there are others—mainly fans of bigger government—who say the Constitution is "a living and breathing document" that must adapt to give the government the power it "needs" to "solve" our changing problems. They feel the meanings of the words in the Constitution are "elastic" and can be reinterpreted with the changing times.

Apparently, the simple power to amend the Constitution isn't enough for them . . . it's just too, well, inconvenient.

In 2011, Richard Stengel, managing editor of *Time* magazine and former president and chief executive officer of the National Constitution Center, wrote a cover story for *Time* titled "One Document, Under Siege," detailing how the Constitution wasn't actually a limiting document for government. He said that the founders intended its meaning to be interpreted loosely with the changing times to allow government the power to do whatever was "necessary." Stengel argued:

> Here are a few things the framers did not know about: World War II. DNA. Sexting. Airplanes. The atom. Television. Medicare. Collateralized debt obligations. The germ theory of disease. Miniskirts. The internal combustion engine. Computers. Antibiotics. Lady Gaga.
>
> If the Constitution was intended to limit the federal government, it sure doesn't say so. Article I, Section 8, the longest section of the longest article of the Constitution, is a drumroll of congressional power. And it ends with the "necessary and proper" clause, which delegates to Congress the power "to make all laws which shall be necessary and proper for carrying into Execution the foregoing Powers, and all other powers vested by this Constitution in the Government of the United States, or in any Department or Officer thereof." Limited government indeed.

Stengel's recitation of part of the Necessary and Proper Clause above—rather than making the case for unlimited powers as he says it does—actually reinforces the fact that Congress can *only* make laws relative to the limited list of powers delegated to it in the Constitution.

As I discussed in chapter 2, the framers of the Constitution were clearly hesitant to create a list of the people's rights—a bill of rights—because those rights were too numerous and almost indefinite to contain in any document. However, the framers were not at all hesitant to clearly delineate in the Constitution a list of powers for the federal government, because they agreed they should be limited. The framers frequently pointed out in their correspondence and in the very documents that were used to convince people to ratify the Constitution—the *Federalist Papers*—that one way to assure the limitation of the government's powers was to enumerate, or list, them.

Stengel went on to advocate that the meaning of the Constitution has to be forever changing, allowing more power to accumulate to Washington, or else we risk the Constitution's standing in the way of big-government "progress":

> The Constitution works so well precisely because it is so opaque, so general, so open to various interpretations. . . . We can pat ourselves on the back about the past 223 years, but we cannot let the Constitution become an obstacle to the U.S.'s moving into the future with a sensible health care system, a globalized economy, an evolving sense of civil and political rights.

Stengel was at least civil about putting forward his point of view. Others, like *Washington Post* op-ed columnist Richard Cohen, were just plain nasty and, frankly, shared their views before they had any true grasp of what they were talking about:

> This fatuous infatuation with the Constitution, particularly the 10th Amendment, is clearly the work of witches, wiccans and wackos. It has nothing to do with America's real problems and, if taken too seriously, would cause an

economic and political calamity. The Constitution is a wonderful document, quite miraculous actually, but only because it has been wisely adapted to changing times. To adhere to the very word of its every clause hardly is respectful to the Founding Fathers. They were revolutionaries who embraced change. That's how we got here.

"To adhere to the very word of its every clause hardly is respectful to the Founding Fathers"? Incredible! In Cohen's view, the Constitution is merely a list of suggestions. I wonder if the op-ed columnist accepts such a loose interpretation of the Constitution that he believes the government doesn't really have to keep its hands off his First Amendment rights as well.

The Constitution isn't perfect. The men who wrote it weren't perfect—in fact, they had many disagreements over it, and many parts of it were written as compromises. Humble enough to recognize that, they created a way to change it, if the people deemed it necessary.

Yes, the Constitution is meant to evolve with changing times and a growing nation, but the evolution is supposed to occur through the *amendment process,* whereby constitutional amendments go through a long and deliberative process involving Congress and at least three-fourths of the states. Changes to the Constitution are not supposed to happen by changing the meaning of words in the *existing text* simply because the president, or a majority of those in Congress, or five justices on the Supreme Court decide by themselves that the Constitution as written doesn't fit their policy objectives.

Think of the Constitution as a contract between the people and their government, setting up the rules about how the government will act on their behalf in exchange for the people's granting it limited authority to carry out those actions.

Think about what would happen if this loose interpretation of words that Stengel and others advocate happened with other contracts the way it does with the Constitution. What if a court could redefine the words in your job contract, your mortgage contract, or your auto loan at any time, raising your interest rates or cutting your pay just because the court thought that would serve a better purpose? Who would agree to be bound by a contract like that?

Words in contracts do not take on new meanings just because the years go by. If you want to change a contract, you have to amend it by an agreement of all parties involved. The same principle applies to the Constitution: if you want to change what the Constitution means, you need to go through the constitutional amendment process. One reason government has become so massive and out of control is because those in Washington decided on their own, outside of that process, to reinterpret the meaning of words over the years, and the Supreme Court has both acquiesced in, and itself accomplished, such "reinterpretations." As a result, those in Washington have been able to give the federal government expanded powers we citizens never intended it to have.

No one can feel secure in the law if the definitions of words are changeable. If the Constitution is malleable and subject to wide interpretation, that means that our liberty is subject to interpretation, too. As James Madison said in 1824:

> I entirely concur in the propriety of resorting to the sense in which the Constitution was accepted and ratified by the nation. . . . What a metamorphosis would be produced in the code of law if all its ancient phraseology were to be taken in its modern sense.

The Criticisms over Suing the Federal Government

BEING IN POLITICS, I am constantly surprised at how stunningly risk-averse people become once they get elected. They may get

84

elected railing on unnecessary tax increases, government waste, too many onerous regulations, or the poor performance of government programs. But once they're elected, they decide that eliminating that government program or that regulation is a little too risky, because there's some group of voters (who probably won't vote for them anyway) who'll be angry and vocal about it if they do.

I've seen too many politicians whose new primary purpose once they get elected is simply to get reelected, instead of working for all those reasons they originally campaigned for when running for office.

When I was asked by the *Richmond Times-Dispatch* in 2011 why I get in these federalism fights like the ones over Obamacare and with the EPA despite the beatings I may take from some in the media and those on the Left, I told the paper what I had told voters for years: "I'm willing to lose. I fight hard to win. . . . But I'm not afraid to lose. I can walk away after the next election a happy man. I have a real sense I have a role to play. I have a purpose to my role in political contests and it is to pursue the vision of the Founders in the 21st century."

On the other hand, nobody wants to be seen as suing good old "Uncle Sam." But my coauthor, Brian Gottstein, put it this way: "Uncle Sam wouldn't do what they're trying to do to the Constitution. They're not Uncle Sam. They're holding Uncle Sam hostage. It's our job to try to save him."

By engaging in the federalism fights over health care and the overreach of the EPA, the FCC, the National Labor Relations Board, and others, I was just doing what I had promised when I campaigned for office. Even politicians on the other side of the aisle acknowledged that. "Ken's doing exactly what he said he'd do," Virginia delegate Scott Surovell, a Democrat, told the *Washingtonian.*

Scott went on to say, "[B]ut nobody was paying attention to it when he ran." Which I read to mean, "No one believed he'd really do this."

When I ran for attorney general, I said that when the federal government overstepped its bounds, I would fight back. Unfortunately for Virginians and for the American people in general, the Obama administration gave me more opportunities than I would have liked to keep that promise . . . but I kept it.

I still have people come up to me excitedly saying, "I can't believe you're doing exactly what you said during your campaign!" I don't know whether to be flattered or offended, but as a frustrated voter myself, I understood the sentiment.

I think a lot of big-government activists and those in the more leftist spectrum of the media are used to being able to shout down conservatives, and many politicians just end up cowering. When I don't do that, it just makes them all the angrier. That's why when they criticized the states' lawsuits against the federal government, I didn't cower. Instead, I used those moments as opportunities to directly confront their objections and further educate the public about the fundamental principles for which we were fighting . . . and why they should try to influence that fight, too.

When Virginia brought its health care suit in 2010, the political and left-leaning media attack dogs were let loose, and I was accused of launching an ideological campaign to satisfy my conservative base and to pad my résumé for future political office. Despite the fact that the Virginia Health Care Freedom Act was passed with an *overwhelming majority* of Democrat support in the Virginia General Assembly, and the fact that part of the attorney general's job is to defend Virginia laws in court when they're challenged, many Democrat leaders in the state criticized me for taking the case and accused me of wasting taxpayer dollars to do it.

I was doing my job, carrying out my sworn duty to uphold the Constitution, *and* defending a law that *they* had passed, but few seemed to acknowledge the hypocrisy of the Democrat leadership. Curiously, it also seemed to be one of the few times that Democrat leaders actually cared about the efficient use of taxpayer dollars. The irony was not lost on me that the same people who felt that the federal government should go trillions of dollars into debt by spending more on social programs and corporate bailouts were all of a sudden feeling thrifty over a few thousand dollars spent on a lawsuit they didn't like.

I hadn't previously heard any concerns from that same group about the amount of taxpayer money my office spent in our lawsuits against private defendants, such as banks, manufacturers, and marketing companies. It was obvious that the real issue wasn't that my critics disapproved of me going after lawbreakers; it was that they didn't like me going after this particular lawbreaker: the federal government.

Several media editorial boards were glad to echo the sentiment that the case was a waste of taxpayer money, and some reporters rushed to find "legal scholars" who would denounce the suit as foolhardy and who would discredit our legal arguments. They found one law professor who said that the states' arguments about the constitutionality of the health insurance mandate were, "if not frivolous, close to it."

Frivolous lawsuits don't beat back the federal government's attempts to get them dismissed. Frivolous lawsuits don't win in courts around the country—including our case in Richmond, Virginia. And frivolous lawsuits don't get three days of hearings at the United States Supreme Court, as the health care case eventually did.

Another so-called legal expert said our case relied on a "controversial reading of the Constitution." This comment was my personal favorite. Apparently, we had reached the point where it was controversial to apply the Constitution as it was written! Frankly, I didn't know how anyone who had studied law could say that it was controversial to apply the Constitution as it was written. But many did.

Freedom of Information Act requests inundated my office from newsrooms and Democrat operatives looking for how much money had been spent and how many lawyers were working on the suit. It was the largest flood of requests the Virginia attorney general's office had ever seen. The irony was that it seemed as if it took more time to answer the requests than it took to write the legal briefs and argue the case in court.

Despite the disingenuous attacks over how much money was spent on the lawsuit, I certainly took the use of taxpayers' dollars seriously. The costs for the suit were relatively small because members of my senior staff and I—who were already on the payroll—handled the litigation almost entirely ourselves. There were no outside law firms brought in. And since the case was centered on a purely legal constitutional argument, there were no costs for things such as discovery, witnesses, and the like. The only real expenses were court filing fees, printing fees, transcription fees, and postage, which totaled a little more than $22,000 *over two and a half years.*

The real cost would have been to not even attempt to stop the federal government's constitutional violations—an even greater cost to society that couldn't be measured in dollars, but instead in the loss of freedom. Whether the states ultimately won or lost, the federal government would at least know that it couldn't just violate the Constitution or break federal laws with impunity.

Because our critics couldn't get us on the "wasting taxpayer dollars" front, they kept coming after us on other fronts. I was accused of being partisan and of opposing Obamacare only because it was a Democrat initiative. In prior congresses, Republicans and even conservative policy wonks had floated the idea of a health insurance mandate, too, as part of a plan for health care reform, calling it an issue of personal responsibility and a way to avoid a government-sponsored insurance system.

But the idea was just as terrible and unconstitutional when Republicans brought it up. Fortunately, they never passed a mandate. If a Republican president and Congress had passed this mandate in 2010, we still would have challenged it. The bottom line is that protecting limited-government principles and individual liberty shouldn't be partisan issues.

In fact, in 2011 when five Republicans in the U.S. Senate proposed Senate Bill 197—dictating how *state* courts must handle medical malpractice lawsuits as a way to cut health care costs—I openly warned the senators that what they were attempting was unconstitutional, and that if they succeeded in passing their legislation, we would challenge it in court.

As a state attorney general struggling to hold back a flood of impositions by the Obama administration that violated federal law or the Constitution, I was disappointed to see Republicans trampling the states' prerogatives in our constitutional system in the same way as the administration and its allies.

While I have long been concerned that our legal system encouraged more lawsuits than were appropriate, and I understood that out-of-control medical malpractice awards led to higher medical costs, I didn't think any Republican should have been willing to violate the Constitution to try to solve the problem. I believe Republicans need to be the guardians of the Constitution and of limited-government principles—not just because it's the right thing to do, but because if they don't play that role in our government, who will?

There were other criticisms that emerged over the case, including one that the Republican attorneys general were just "in bed" with the insurance industry. This criticism really defied all logic. The individual mandate was the one piece of the federal health care law that the health insurance companies loved. When the government ordered every uninsured American to buy private health insurance, it guaranteed the insurance companies a flood of new customers beginning in 2014.

E-mails between the White House and drug companies, insurance companies, and other special interests surfaced, showing that many of these big companies were "in bed" with President Obama and members of Congress about the details of the bill.

Are you surprised? I didn't think so . . .

More Criticism: The Insidious
"States' Rights" Race Card

FOR ABOUT THE first year of the health care suit, we were constantly battling the notion that we were fighting for "nullification" or "states' rights"—labels I didn't use myself. Those on the Left intentionally tried to assign those labels to us because it was loaded language that carried a lot of baggage from the 1950s and '60s, when standing up for "states' rights" against the federal government meant you were against civil rights and integration for black people.

One sure sign that the Left doesn't have a good, substantive argument is that they play the race card.

The race card was especially troubling for those of us in the southern states because we were accused of wanting to fight the Civil War all over again. It was also extremely bad timing, as 2011 was the year Virginia began to commemorate the 150th anniversary of the Civil War. Our opponents tried to paint our health care lawsuit as just one more attempt in a long line of attempts—from secession, to the Civil War, to the 1960s states' rights push-back against integration—for the South to rise again, all in an attempt to delegitimize what we were really fighting for.

The *Baltimore Sun* managed to fit both the Civil War and the civil rights slams in the same piece when it editorialized the day after the lawsuits were filed:

> Yet again, conservatives are falling on a 10th Amendment "states' rights" claim when they don't care for progressive actions at the federal level. The argument is as old as the Civil War and is commonly trotted out when public outrage (think the 1964 Civil Rights Act) is at its highest.

Then–*New York Times* columnist Frank Rich wrote:

> The state attorneys general who are invoking states'
> rights in their lawsuits to nullify the federal health care
> law are transparently pushing the same old hot buttons.
>
> "They tried it here in Arkansas in '57, and it didn't
> work," said the Democratic governor of that state, Mike
> Beebe, likening the states' health care suits to the failed
> effort of his predecessor Orval Faubus to block nine black
> students from attending the all-white Little Rock Central
> High School.

And *Washington Post* columnist E. J. Dionne Jr. said that the "attack" on health care reform would bring us back to the 1830s:

> [The lawsuit] reveals how far into the past America's
> New Nullifiers want to push the nation. They don't just
> want to abandon a seven-plus-decade understanding of
> the Constitution's interstate commerce clause that has al-
> lowed the federal government to regulate a modern, na-
> tional economy. They also want to resurrect states' rights
> doctrines discredited by President Andrew Jackson dur-
> ing the Nullification Crisis of the 1830s and buried by the
> Civil War.

By the way, contrary to Frank Rich's and E. J. Dionne's assess-
ments, these lawsuits weren't "nullification." Many like Rich and
Dionne tried to label the states' approach as nullification, but they
clearly didn't know what they were talking about. Nullification is the
idea that a state has the power to refuse to follow a federal law that it
deems unconstitutional and, therefore, is "null and void" within its

borders. In the past, nullification has led to threats of armed conflict between the states and the federal government.

In the health care case, the states were prepared to follow the law if it were ultimately declared constitutional. At the same time, we were going to try our hardest to challenge its constitutionality in the federal government's *own* courts.

That wasn't nullification; that was following constitutional design.

CHAPTER 5

"BECAUSE I SAID SO" AND OTHER
PROFOUND LEGAL ARGUMENTS

||||||||||||||||||||||||||||||||||||||||||||||||||||||||||||||||||||||||||||||||||||||||||||||||||||||||||

*How strangely will the Tools of a Tyrant pervert
the plain Meaning of Words!*

—SAMUEL ADAMS, 1776, American revolutionary
and organizer of the Boston Tea Party

If the Mandate Argument Doesn't Look Like
It's Working, Just Call It a Tax Instead

AFTER THREE MONTHS of trading arguments with Virginia about the individual-insurance mandate through legal briefs, in its first court appearance on July 1, 2010, the Obama administration began to look as if it wasn't even convinced of its own Commerce Clause argument. Instead, it started to argue a second, fallback position in the Richmond courtroom: lawyers for the administration argued for the first time that the penalty for not buying health insurance was actually *not* a penalty at all; instead, they said, it was a new "tax."

This sudden change in their argument was surprising, because it was in stark contrast to what was said in the debates over the health care bill before it was signed into law. Democrats in Congress and President Obama had adamantly insisted the $695 annual penalty for not having government-approved health insurance was a penalty and not a tax. In fact, the president was especially emphatic about this point in September 2009, when on *This Week with George Stephanopou-los*, he argued with Mr. Stephanopoulos over it:

STEPHANOPOULOS: Under this mandate, the government
   is forcing people to spend money, fining you if you don't.
   How is that not a tax?

OBAMA: Well, hold on a second, George. Here—here's
   what's happening.
       . . . We're giving tax credits, we've set up an exchange,
   you are now part of a big pool, we've driven down the
   costs, we've done everything we can and you actually
   can afford health insurance, but you've just decided, you
   know what, I want to take my chances. And then you get
   hit by a bus and you and I have to pay for the emergency
   room care, that's—

STEPHANOPOULOS: That may be, but it's still a tax increase.

OBAMA: No. That's not true, George. The—for us to say
   that you've got to take a responsibility to get health
   insurance is absolutely not a tax increase. What it's
   saying is, is that we're not going to have other people
   carrying your burdens for you anymore than the fact
   that right now everybody in America, just about, has
   to get auto insurance. Nobody considers that a tax
   increase. . . .

OBAMA: No, but—but, George, you—you can't just make
   up that language and decide that that's called a tax
   increase. . . .

STEPHANOPOULOS: . . . But your critics say it is a tax
   increase.

OBAMA: My critics say everything is a tax increase. My
   critics say that I'm taking over every sector of the
   economy. You know that. Look, we can have a legitimate

debate about whether or not we're going to have an
individual mandate or not, but—

STEPHANOPOULOS: But you reject that it's a tax increase?

OBAMA: I absolutely reject that notion.

Of course, it made sense for the president to argue that the mandate was a mandate and not a tax, since he had repeatedly pledged not
to raise taxes on the middle class. "If you are a family making less than
$250,000 a year, you will not see your taxes go up" was a promise often
repeated by Mr. Obama when campaigning in 2008.

Moreover, we were in the middle of one of the worst economic
downturns in American history. Lower- and middle-class Americans
were losing their jobs and their homes, and a new $1 trillion health
care tax would certainly turn voters against the president and Congress. But a "penalty" on those "so selfish" as to not want to participate in a program that provided "health care for all" would easily
gain approval from the Democrat voting base and a Democrat-led
Congress. Lacking the guts to pass the taxes needed to pay for their
new entitlement program, Congress passed a mandate structured as a
penalty.

But now that the federal courts were willing to hear challenges
to the mandate and it looked as if some judges might agree that it
was unconstitutional to force people to buy a private product, the administration's lawyers threw the tax argument into the mix to attempt
to save PPACA. They tried to convince the courts that the mandate
was merely a legal exercise of Congress's constitutional *taxing* power.
Remember that taxing people to pay for a health care program would
have been constitutional.

Once again, the Obama administration argued that the plain
meaning of words really didn't mean what everyone understood them
to mean: according to the administration, not only was inactivity really
activity, but penalties were now really taxes.

Noah Webster would have been appalled. Apparently, no one in Washington owned a dictionary. It reminded me of another president who tried to get around the law, too, when he said, "It depends on what the meaning of the word 'is' is."

Although the Commerce Clause mandate argument advanced by the federal government was overreaching and unprecedented, this taxing power argument was simply radical.

While many people initially didn't seem to care about this distinction between taxes and penalties, Virginia was adamant that this was not just some academic point, and we weren't willing to concede it to the feds. We argued that the government couldn't arbitrarily change the definition of words and start calling a penalty a tax to try to make the mandate appear constitutional, for the following reasons:

- The health care law had already been *written* as a mandate and *passed* as a mandate.
- A penalty for inaction is not a tax of any kind allowed under the Constitution.
- Congress itself called the penalty for not buying insurance a "penalty" and explicitly claimed authority to create it *only* under the Commerce Clause, never under its taxing authority.
- In other parts of PPACA, Congress levied taxes and called them "taxes," demonstrating that it knew how to draw the distinction between taxes and penalties.
- In an earlier version of the bill, Congress had actually used the word *tax* but chose to amend it to *penalty*. Congress made a very conscious decision between whether it was a "tax" or a "penalty," and it chose "penalty."

For the lawyers from the Justice Department to make their argument, they had to ignore the very words that Congress chose to use when writing the law.

As another matter, penalties and taxes function in different ways. A penalty is a threat used to alter conduct, and if that conduct is altered, the penalty won't be collected. A tax, on the other hand, is used explicitly to raise revenue. In the case of PPACA, if the penalty worked as planned, it would raise little revenue for the government because people would follow the mandate to avoid paying the penalty. Penalties and taxes serve two different functions, and the two terms can't be used interchangeably.

During the July 2010 hearing in federal court in Richmond, Judge Henry Hudson appeared annoyed with the federal government's tax argument. After the first time the lawyer for the Obama administration asserted that the mandate penalty "is a tax," Judge Hudson interrupted him, challenging him:

> Why then is [the individual mandate] prefaced by saying that it is an exercise of Commerce Clause power? Why did the members of Congress, as well as the president, deny to every person in America that it was not a tax? Was it just tacking to the political winds at the time, or did it have substance to it?

Later, Judge Hudson asked:

> [I]n the House Bill, which was passed first, they referred to it . . . as a tax. . . . And the only way it could pass the Senate was for the word "tax" to be struck and the word "penalty" put in so that it would be consistent with the representations that both the president and Congress made to the American people. Does that have any significance at all?

And later still, appearing fed up with the dodgy answers from the federal government's lawyer, Judge Hudson interjected, asking pointedly:

> Now let's characterize it correctly. They denied it was a
> tax. The president denied it. Was he trying to deceive
> the people in doing that?

I can't overstate how extraordinary these exchanges were. Judge Hudson was not alone in his consternation with the duplicity of the federal government. Given Congress's and the president's repeated denials that they were exercising the taxing power, federal judges were in a very awkward position when the federal government sauntered into court asserting, "Of course it's a tax!"

Even if the Justice Department could overcome these logical hurdles, the United States Supreme Court had long recognized that taxes and penalties were separate and distinct and had distinguished that a tax was a forced contribution to provide for the support of government, while a penalty was imposed as punishment for breaking the law.

For example, in the 1931 case of *United States v. La Franca*, the Supreme Court held that the words *tax* and *penalty* "are not interchangeable, one for the other. No mere exercise of the art of lexicography can alter the essential nature of an act or a thing; and if an exaction be clearly a penalty it cannot be converted into a tax by the simple expedient of calling it such. That the exaction here in question is not a true tax, but a penalty involving the idea of punishment for infraction of the law is settled." That precedent was pretty tough to argue against, but the Justice Department would give it a try anyway.

Twisting the meaning of words yet again, Justice Department lawyers tried to argue to Judge Hudson that breaking a criminal law was an unlawful act, but that breaking a civil law *wasn't*, and therefore, when the Supreme Court had previously talked about penalties for "unlawful acts," unlawful acts just referred to *criminal* violations, not civil violations. They argued that the penalties for violating civil laws (which the PPACA mandate was) weren't really penalties at all, so the Supreme Court precedent didn't apply.

But that simply was not the law. The idea that it was only "unlawful" to violate criminal laws as opposed to civil laws was absurd and a legal fiction that the federal government had pulled out of thin air . . . or somewhere worse.

Even if the courts bought the argument that the penalty was a tax, a simple understanding of the Constitution and past Supreme Court precedent had affirmed that Congress couldn't create a tax for the primary purpose of getting around the Constitution—that is, to create a tax so it could regulate something that it didn't explicitly have the constitutional authority to regulate. For example, if the federal government doesn't have the authority under the Constitution to make you eat peanut butter and jelly sandwiches, it's not allowed to get around that prohibition by penalizing you through the creation of a tax for not eating peanut butter and jelly sandwiches. That tax would really be just a veiled penalty to regulate behavior rather than to raise revenue.

If the federal government could get around the Constitution that way, it would have a virtually unlimited authority to regulate any behavior it wanted—even behavior it was prohibited from regulating— merely by creating new taxes.

For the courts that heard the challenges to PPACA to have accepted that the penalty was a tax would have required the courts to ignore Supreme Court precedent and effectively rewrite PPACA as a tax, which they had no authority to do, especially after Congress had already explicitly amended it to *not* be a tax. As a matter of separation of powers, remember, only Congress can write (and rewrite) laws. (Note that this is not-so-subtle foreshadowing. But don't jump ahead to the chapter detailing the Supreme Court decision.)

Fortunately, every federal district and appeals court that ruled on the government's flip-flopping tax argument refused to accept it.

Every single one. Perhaps the administration's legal team should have remembered the president's own words on *This Week* when he said, "[Y]ou can't just make up that language and decide that that's called a tax increase."

If the "Mandate" and "Tax" Arguments Don't Look Like They're Working, Let's Resort to the "It's for the Good of Society" Argument

FACED WITH THE legal obstacles of trying to force people to buy private insurance under a dubious Commerce Clause mandate and then flip-flopping between whether the mandate penalty was actually a penalty or a tax, supporters of PPACA often made arguments that weren't based on the Constitution or the law. The most common argument was that because America had a pressing national problem it needed to address, PPACA must be constitutional because it addressed that problem.

In other words, it didn't matter what the law was or what the Constitution said; the issue needed to be solved, and the ends justified the means. That's the kind of lawless thinking of dictators and despots, but that was becoming the thinking of some of our fellow citizens. The disappointing part was that we also heard this argument from the very people in Congress whom we entrusted to be our leaders and to make our laws . . . and who also swore an oath to uphold the Constitution.

In *New York v. United States* in 1992, the Supreme Court warned about the dangers of giving the government new powers beyond its authority out of good intentions:

> But the Constitution protects us from our own best in-
> tentions: It divides power among sovereigns and among
> branches of government precisely so that we may resist

the temptation to concentrate power in one location as an expedient solution to the crisis of the day. . . . [Something may be a] pressing national problem, but a judiciary that licensed extraconstitutional government with each issue of comparable gravity would, in the long run, be far worse.

While well-intentioned, expedient government solutions may solve our problems temporarily, the loss of liberty in the process may be permanent. Remember Thomas Friedman's admiration of the expediency of the Chinese government over American republicanism? Would you really want to trade the American system for one like China's Communist state?

Should the Whole Obamacare Law—or Just the Individual Mandate—Be Struck Down?

ANOTHER QUESTION THE courts had to contend with was, if they found the individual-insurance mandate to be unconstitutional, should they strike down all of Obamacare, or just the mandate and the parts that relied on it?

A curious thing to note was that the final version of the health care law didn't contain a severance clause, even though an earlier version of the bill did.

Severance clauses are often contained in contracts and large, multipart laws. With laws, such a clause is used to ensure that a law can still stand even if it contains a part that a court deems violates the Constitution. A severance clause allows the unconstitutional section to be "severed" and removed from the law and thrown out, leaving the rest of the law in force.

Why didn't PPACA contain a typical severance clause? No one

outside of the bill drafters seemed to know for sure, because no one had ever taken responsibility for not including it. But I have two possible theories. The most likely theory seemed to be that in their rush to ram a bill that was hundreds of pages long down America's throat before anyone could read it, the Democrats just plain forgot to include a severance clause. My second theory is that all the different special interests involved in writing the bill behind closed doors—Senator Reid, Speaker Pelosi, President Obama, drug companies, insurance companies, and others—had struck a bargain that included mutually assured destruction: if one group's special piece of the law was thrown out, they wanted the whole law thrown out.

The lack of a severance clause gave many people hope that the entire law could be struck down automatically if the mandate were found unconstitutional. But that was a misconception. Even in the absence of a severance clause, a judge generally prefers not to strike down a whole law, but instead will try to sever out the offending part, along with all the other parts that couldn't function properly without it.

The alternative to severing is called the "legislative bargain" theory. In those instances in which the offending part is so central to the law that the law would never have passed without it (an all-or-nothing deal), the proper course is for a judge to strike the entire law. Otherwise, by taking out one part and leaving the others, a judge would be rewriting the law in a way that the legislature never intended, and in a way that would have never passed in the first place. In essence, the judge would be creating his or her own version of the law (just as if he were to rewrite the mandate as a tax—more foreshadowing), when that's solely the job of the legislative branch.

Virginia's position was that Obamacare was a perfect case of the "legislative bargain" theory in action. We argued that the federal health care law would never have passed Congress without the individual mandate; therefore, any judge should strike down the entire law. And frankly, if the courts agreed that the mandate was unconstitutional, imagine how unbelievably difficult it would have been for them to go through the hundreds of pages of the law to determine which parts should have been severed because they were dependent on the mandate.

There were a couple of reasons we knew that the health care law would have never passed Congress without the individual mandate. The first reason was the one you already know: because Congress didn't want to be accused of passing one of the biggest tax increases in American history, it passed a mandate instead. The second reason was that the parts of the law that Congress itself declared were the most important would not have worked without an individual-insurance mandate.

Virginia used the federal government's own words against it in this second regard. The Obama administration said in its court briefs that the health insurance mandate (the "minimum essential coverage provision," as the law called it) was the "linchpin" of the entire law. The lawyers for the government repeatedly and steadfastly maintained that the law was *unworkable* without it.

In their court arguments, the federal government argued, "What Congress found, and what the testimony before Congress was, the market would go into extinction or it would implode. [The mandate] actually was *essential* to make the reforms work."

"Essential"!

In its court filings, the federal government also said, "Congress determined that, without the minimum coverage provision [the mandate], the reforms in the Act . . . would not work."

Even in the law itself, Congress explicitly stated that the mandate and penalty were "*essential* to creating effective health insurance markets in which improved health insurance products that are guaranteed issue and do not exclude coverage of preexisting conditions can be sold." (Under the PPACA law, "guaranteed issue" meant that insurance companies were forced to accept applicants with preexisting conditions.)

So PPACA's defenders admitted that the mandate wasn't severable from the rest of the law. If the mandate went down, the whole law should go down with it.

Why Was the Mandate Critical to the Law Functioning Properly?

HOW TO HANDLE preexisting conditions was one of the most difficult policy issues in health care reform.

Before PPACA was passed, insurance companies—being businesses and not charities—had previously denied or delayed coverage to people with certain expensive preexisting medical conditions or had charged prohibitively expensive premiums for covering them. While being denied coverage was extremely unfortunate for people with these conditions, it wasn't an evil plot by insurance companies that hated sick people; rather, it was a business decision to keep from losing money, going out of business, and leaving even more people uninsured as a result. The insurance companies had calculated that they might not collect enough in premiums from people with preexisting conditions to cover the costs of all the medicines and treatments they knew those policyholders would inevitably need over their lifetimes.

PPACA forced insurance companies to accept applicants with preexisting conditions. The law also barred insurance companies from charging higher premiums to those with preexisting conditions, requiring insurers to use a "community rating" process to price their insurance policies relatively equally.

By itself, the legal guarantee that people couldn't be denied coverage or couldn't be charged more because of preexisting conditions would have allowed them to wait to buy health insurance until *after* they became sick or injured, as they would have no rational economic incentive to buy insurance beforehand and pay all those premiums in advance. These "free riders," as the PPACA proponents called them, would have paid nothing in but would be immediately eligible to receive benefits. To prevent this free-rider problem, the government created the mandate to force everyone to buy health insurance whether they wanted it or not.

Additionally, the health care law removed payout caps that insurance companies had previously imposed to limit the amount of benefits they paid out per policyholder over the course of a year or over a policyholder's lifetime. Although this, too, was unfortunate, and some people with very expensive medical conditions would hit their policy caps and no longer be eligible for private coverage, insurance companies couldn't routinely pay out more money than they took in. And while insurance was meant to spread risk over large pools of healthy and unhealthy people, other policyholders didn't exist simply for the purpose of paying higher premiums to subsidize people who paid thousands of dollars in premiums but took out millions of dollars in benefits. That would be utterly unsustainable.

Insurance companies had to manage risk by not overexposing themselves to large numbers of sick people who were virtually guaranteed to take more out of the insurance pool than they would ever contribute. Again, if insurance companies couldn't manage their risks this way, they would have to raise premiums even more and put health insurance out of the reach of even more people, or they would hemorrhage money and go out of business. Then, instead of a small percentage of people who couldn't get coverage, *no one* would get coverage.

Since the federal health care law outlawed these payout caps and exposed insurance companies to much greater financial risk, mandating that everyone buy health insurance was intended to widen the pool of policyholders to spread the costs over a wider group. This way, more healthy people would pay premiums while presumably needing little medical care, which forced them to subsidize the cost of covering more sick people with more expensive needs. Under the Obamacare scheme, unless everyone was forced into the insurance pool, there wouldn't be enough money to cover everybody.

Of course, as I said before, the mandate requiring everyone to buy insurance would have been entirely unnecessary if Congress had had the political will to pass Obamacare as a tax in the first place. Then it could have used the taxes it raised to fund a special insurance account for people with preexisting conditions, people who had exceeded their policy caps, and people who couldn't afford coverage at all. But again, the congressional Democrats and the president were worried more about their own political futures than they were about being honest with the American people.

CHAPTER 6

TAKING THE OFFENSIVE
. . . AND WINNING

|||||||||||||||||||||||||||||||||||||||||||||||||||||||||||||||||||||||||||||||||||||||||||||||||||||||||||||||||

I consider the foundation of the Constitution as laid on this ground that "all powers not delegated to the United States, by the Constitution, nor prohibited by it to the states, are reserved to the states or to the people." To take a single step beyond the boundaries thus specially drawn around the powers of Congress, is to take possession of a boundless field of power, not longer susceptible of any definition.

—THOMAS JEFFERSON, 1791

The First Win Against Obamacare

BY DECEMBER 2010, at least a dozen challenges to the health care law had already been thrown out of federal courts, and in two other challenges, two federal judges had upheld the law as constitutional (U.S. district court judge George Steeh in Michigan in *Thomas More Law Center v. Obama* and U.S. district court judge Norman Moon in Virginia in *Liberty University v. Geithner*).

On the morning of December 13, 2010, just hours before federal district court judge Henry Hudson handed down his ruling in our case, *Commonwealth of Virginia v. Kathleen Sebelius*, I prepared my senior staff for a potential court loss. I told them that our job wasn't necessarily to win, because we didn't have control over whether we would win. Instead, I told them that our job was to fight as hard as we could, because in cases like these, we always could—and always would—fight.

While we were prepared for a loss, on that December 13 morning, Judge Hudson ruled in Virginia's favor, declaring the individual-insurance mandate unconstitutional. Virginia had been the first state to argue in federal court that the law was unconstitutional, and now it was the first plaintiff to secure a win against Obamacare and establish a successful argument against the mandate.

In his ruling, Judge Hudson stated:

> Despite the laudable intentions of Congress in enacting a comprehensive and transformative health care regime, the legislative process must still operate within constitutional bounds. Salutatory goals and creative drafting have never been sufficient to offset an absence of enumerated powers. . . .
>
> At its core, this dispute is not simply about regulating the business of insurance—or crafting a scheme of universal health insurance coverage—it's about an individual's right to choose to participate.

The judge held that the individual mandate and penalty were "neither within the letter nor spirit of the Constitution" and that the mandate "exceeds the constitutional boundaries of congressional power." He concurred with Virginia that the power Congress was claiming was absolutely unprecedented. Never had the courts "extended Commerce Clause powers to compel an individual to involuntarily enter the stream of commerce by purchasing a commodity in the private market," he said.

In its arguments, the federal government had asserted that "everyone" at some point in his or her lifetime would eventually need health care services and would therefore enter the health care market-place (in other words, "everyone" would enter into this stream of commerce), and since people generally couldn't predict when that would be, the Commerce Clause allowed the government to force them to buy insurance in advance to ensure they were prepared for entering the marketplace. In response, Judge Hudson disputed that interpretation of the Commerce Clause, arguing that "the same reasoning could apply to transportation, housing, or nutritional decisions," allowing the government to dictate what you drove, the size of the house you lived in, or what you ate.

The judge also rejected the administration's argument that the penalty was actually a tax and that Congress's taxing power gave it the authority to impose a penalty on those who didn't buy insurance. He said the administration had avoided using the word *tax* during the debate over the law's passage, and was now only employing the word to try to give the mandate legal legitimacy. Because the penalty would raise so much less than Obamacare would actually cost, he concluded the penalty "lacks a bona fide intention to raise revenue"—the real definition of a tax.

However, Judge Hudson also concluded that the unconstitutional individual mandate *could* be severed from the rest of the law, and he only struck down the mandate and any provisions that were directly dependent on it, while leaving the rest of the law intact. As a result, he denied our request for an injunction that would have stopped the law from being implemented.

While this first win was encouraging, it was only the first step in a multistep process. We knew from the day we filed our lawsuit that whichever side lost would undoubtedly appeal to the next court and then to the next; and that scenario would be repeated with all the lawsuits around the country, until one of them ended up in the U.S. Supreme Court.

A Second Win Against Obamacare

A LITTLE MORE THAN a month after Virginia's win, on January 31, 2011, federal district court judge Roger Vinson handed down the second ruling against Obamacare in Florida's multistate lawsuit, *U.S. Department of Health and Human Services v. Florida.*

The Florida ruling on the individual mandate closely tracked Virginia's ruling. Judge Vinson concluded that the individual mandate was unconstitutional. In what could have easily been the Tea Party movement's favorite quote, the judge said:

> It is difficult to imagine that a nation which began, at least in part, as the result of opposition to a British mandate giving the East India Company a monopoly and imposing a nominal tax on all tea sold in America would have set out to create a government with the power to force people to buy tea in the first place. If Congress can penalize a passive individual for failing to engage in commerce, the enumeration of powers in the Constitution would have been in vain, for it would be difficult to perceive any limitation on federal power.

He also illustrated how far this power could go:

> Congress could require that people buy and consume broccoli at regular intervals, not only because the required purchases will positively impact interstate commerce, but also because people who eat healthier tend to be healthier, and are thus more productive and put less of a strain on the health care system.

Furthermore, he saw that the federal government was attempting to regulate individual thought with the mandate, and he rejected it:

And "decisions" cannot be equated to "activities." Every person throughout the course of his or her life makes hundreds or even thousands of life decisions that involve the same general sort of thought process that the defendants maintain is "economic activity." There will be no stopping point if that should be deemed the equivalent of activity for Commerce Clause purposes.

Judge Vinson also addressed the federal government's assertion that it should be allowed to use its Commerce Clause authority to regulate citizens just because they might have engaged in health care commerce (used health care services) in the past or might someday use them in the future:

The defendants also suggest that the uninsured are "active" in the health insurance market—and therefore can be regulated and forced to buy insurance—because a large percentage of them have had insurance within the past year. The defendants have provided no authority for the suggestion that once someone is in the health insurance market at a particular point in time, they are forever in that market, always subject to regulation, and not ever permitted to leave.

In my office, this is known as the "Hotel California" quote. In the Eagles' song "Hotel California," the eerie lyrics declare, "You can check out at any time you like, but you can never leave."

Having found the individual mandate to be unconstitutional, Judge Vinson then turned to the question of the remedy: whether to strike down the entire law. He found that much of the law relied on the insurance "reforms," which the federal lawyers had already conceded relied on the mandate and penalty. Consequently, he struck down the entire law:

Because the individual mandate is unconstitutional and
not severable, the entire Act must be declared void.

After declaring the entire law to be invalid and of no effect, the
judge asserted that he expected the Obama administration to honor
his ruling—in other words, to cease implementing the law. Not surprisingly, it didn't take the administration that was so accustomed to
ignoring the law very long to start making public statements that it
had no intention of honoring the federal judge's ruling.

Judge Vinson's ruling, however, led a number of *states* to cease
implementing the law until they heard what the U.S. Supreme Court
had to say.

The Medicaid Coercion Issue

THE FLORIDA CASE had another argument in addition to the question of the individual mandate's constitutionality: Medicaid coercion. Medicaid coercion was the attempt by the federal government
to force states to expand their Medicaid programs by threatening to
take away *all* of their federal Medicaid money if they refused to participate in the expansion.

Medicaid is welfare in the form of health care. Medicaid is *not*
health insurance. To get more lower-income Americans health care
coverage, Obamacare forcibly expanded Medicaid eligibility to allow
more people to get on the Medicaid rolls. Although it's a federal
program, the states and the federal government share the costs, so
increasing the number of people on Medicaid would dramatically increase costs not only to the federal government, but to the states as
well.

Many states protested that such an expansion would cost the

states billions of additional dollars each year that they just didn't have. In Virginia alone, estimates showed the expansion could cost taxpayers hundreds of millions of dollars more annually by 2019, as Virginia would have to make up to 420,000 additional residents eligible for Medicaid.

The federal government responded to the protests by proclaiming that if states didn't want to participate in the expansion, their alternative was to get out of the Medicaid program *completely* and give up *all* the federal dollars that went along with it. In most states, this just wasn't a realistic option, because after offering Medicaid for forty-five years, they already had millions of poor citizens dependent on the program even before the Obamacare expansion, and they couldn't afford to keep covering those people with just state dollars. In other words, the government was holding existing Medicaid patients hostage to force the states to buy into the expansion.

To give you a sense of the kind of money we're talking about, let me share a snapshot of Virginia's Medicaid budget with you. About 20 percent of our entire state budget goes to Medicaid. It has been the fastest-growing, hardest-to-control part of our state budget for years. In 2012, Virginia spent about $7.4 billion for Medicaid, with very close to half of that amount—$3.7 billion—coming from the federal government.

Under Obamacare, the feds were threatening to take all $3.7 billion away at once—unless Virginia capitulated and agreed to the Medicaid expansion.

Virginia, like the other states, wasn't in a position to absorb such a sudden and devastating cut. And remember, unlike the federal government, the state governments have to balance their budgets. They don't have the option of endless borrowing to expand programs the way the feds do.

The states in the Florida suit argued that because entirely opting out of Medicaid was unrealistic, the federal government wasn't just offering federal money under its spending power for voluntary acceptance by the states; it was instead illegally coercing the states to participate in the very expensive expansion.

The coercion theory was grounded in a few Supreme Court cases, most recently in *South Dakota v. Dole* in 1987. In that case, the court noted that it was possible that a federal law could be unconstitutional if it were so coercive that it was the equivalent of ordering something be done that was outside of the limited enumerated powers of Congress. The issue in *Dole* was the federal government's withholding of 5 percent of federal highway funds if a state didn't adopt the federal minimum drinking age of twenty-one. The court held that this was a proper use of Congress's spending power because the states were allowed to keep their drinking ages below the federal minimum if they were willing to forego the federal money.

In issuing its decision, however, the court noted that 5 percent of federal highway money was a relatively small amount. The court, relying on cases dating back to the 1930s, noted that there might be a situation in which the amount of money involved were so large that the states would be "forced" into accepting the conditions. If such a situation ever arose, the court indicated that the law might amount to unconstitutional coercion of the states. Though it was theoretically possible, the Supreme Court had never yet found a case in which such coercion existed.

The other problem for the states with this argument was that Medicaid is a voluntary program—states are technically free to participate or not. In other words, the states can pull out at any time. For this reason, the Florida court flatly rejected the states' claim of federal coercion. The court recognized that while a decision not to participate came with significant consequences, those consequences didn't make the federal government's unilateral expansion of Medicaid coercive.

Expediting the Cases to the Supreme Court

THE UNCERTAINTY CAUSED by the divergent rulings of the various federal district courts over Obamacare's constitutionality was having a terrible effect on the economy. Companies had no idea what to project for future health insurance costs for their employees, which made them more reluctant to hire new people. If the health care law were allowed to stand, many employers with more than fifty workers would have to pay a tax of $2,000 or $3,000 per employee under the new law unless they offered a minimum package of "affordable" health benefits at the workplace. Moreover, PPACA mandated that all health insurance plans meet certain minimum standards of coverage to be considered "qualified health plans," but these minimum standards wouldn't be created until later by the U.S. Department of Health and Human Services. Since the standards didn't yet exist, employers had no idea if their existing employee plans would meet the criteria or if they'd have to supplement them with more coverage, which could entail additional unknown costs. Job creation was stagnating because of the ever-increasing uncertainty.

Taxpayers and state legislatures were in a tight situation, too, as state governments with budgets already stretched too thin were faced with spending hundreds of millions of dollars to begin setting up state insurance exchanges to comply with a law that might ultimately be struck down. They were also struggling with how to cope with the enormous increased costs of expanding their Medicaid programs if PPACA were upheld.

And, of course, during this major recession, citizens who didn't have health insurance were looking at their personal budgets to figure out where the heck they were going to find the money to pay for mandated health insurance or the $695 annual penalty for not having it.

The majority of the American people were eager to see the law repealed or ruled unconstitutional. In November 2010, the Republican

Party, which had unanimously opposed PPACA, saw its largest elec-
toral gains in the House of Representatives in more than seventy years.
In January 2011, six additional states joined the Florida multistate suit,
which meant that, for the first time in American history, there was a
majority of states suing the federal government to protect the Constitution. Also in January 2011, the new Republican majority in the
House of Representatives successfully voted to repeal PPACA on a
vote of 245 to 189. And on January 21, Oklahoma's attorney general,
Scott Pruitt, filed suit against Obamacare to enforce a voter-approved
state constitutional amendment that declared its citizens could not be
forced to buy health insurance against their will.

Because of the crippling uncertainty over whether the law would
still be around in two years and the crippling certainty that would
exist if it was, Virginia requested the U.S. Supreme Court do something that it only does on a timeline measured in decades: we asked
the court to expedite the case and skip the appeals courts so we
might be able to get a decision a year sooner. Supreme Court rules
allow the court to immediately review a case "upon a showing that
the case is of such imperative public importance as to justify devia-
tion from normal appellate practice and to require immediate determination." Although I knew it would be a long shot for the justices
to take up our case early, in my mind there was simply too much at
stake to allow the uncertainty to linger and the final resolution to be
unnecessarily delayed.

Furthermore, the case was ready for the court to review. All the
arguments had been extensively laid out by the federal government
and the states in the federal district courts, and we knew the Supreme
Court was going to be the ultimate arbiter of the law's constitutionality. And unlike many other cases, there wasn't much to be developed
at the appeals court level. While we were always sharpening our arguments and our briefs, the fundamental arguments were basically the

same. The arguments that were heard in the district court would essentially be heard all over again.

The Supreme Court had previously granted this type of expedited review in prior cases involving the legality of the federal sentencing guidelines, the reorganization of two railroads, a coal strike, a question of the power of federal courts to enforce rent control, and a constitutional challenge to the Railroad Retirement Act, among others. It seemed that the challenge to the federal health care law had just as much, if not more, public importance.

Because I thought Virginia and our federal opponents would make a clearer, more objective decision about expediting the case before we knew which side had won in district court, my office initiated conversations with the attorneys at the U.S. Department of Justice about fast-tracking the case weeks before the December 2010 ruling came down. I had felt that if both parties in the case appealed to the Supreme Court for expedited review, the likelihood was greater that the justices might take it.

Both supporters and opponents of the law, including Republicans and Democrats, several governors, members of Congress, and other public officials, issued calls for the fast-tracking of our case as well. Virginia's governor, lieutenant governor, and Speaker of the House of Delegates all added their voices to the call. Everyone seemed to understand the gravity of the situation, and many wanted a resolution sooner rather than later—whatever that resolution might be.

But the lawyers for the Obama administration wouldn't make a decision before our December 2010 ruling. It wasn't until *after* the ruling that the Justice Department faxed me a letter conveying its decision *not* to join Virginia in seeking to expedite the case.

So Virginia filed the petition to the Supreme Court on its own. I knew I would take a political hit if the case ended up not getting fast-tracked, as our detractors would eagerly use that as a way to declare we had a loss along the way, especially right after we came off a win in December. But the cost of delay to the commonwealth, its citizens, and its businesses was too great. We had to do the right thing regardless of how it may have looked.

In our petition, we welcomed the court's also expediting the Florida multistate case and all other cases pending in the federal courts of appeals, so that all the key constitutional issues, including Medicaid coercion, could be heard and decided at the same time. It didn't matter which case was heard. What mattered was that the issues needed to be decided as quickly as possible. Every day that passed meant a weaker economy and fewer people going back to work.

Unfortunately, in April 2011, the Supreme Court denied Virginia's petition to call up its case or any other, so we continued to prepare our arguments for the U.S. Court of Appeals for the Fourth Circuit hearing set for May.

With a February 2011 legislative defeat of PPACA repeal efforts in the U.S. Senate, the focus of the fight against Obamacare once again shifted to the courts.

The Next Step: The Circuit Courts of Appeals

I WON'T SPEND A lot of time reviewing the circuit courts of appeals hearings and decisions, as they were merely intermediate steps on the path to the Supreme Court. But I do want to hit some of the highlights, as some parts were very informative, entertaining, and even enraging.

In May 2011, Virginia argued before a three-judge panel of the Fourth Circuit Court of Appeals. Our panel was randomly selected from the fourteen judges on the Fourth Circuit and was comprised of one Clinton appointee and two Obama appointees. That was a tough draw.

During the oral arguments, the federal government seemed downright offended that Virginia was even allowed to bring a lawsuit against it. It was worth being there just to remind the feds that it was the representatives from the *states* who wrote the Constitution that established the federal government in the first place. We were also there to remind them that state cosovereignty with the federal government—that principle of divided government power—was a critical check and balance on federal and state power that helped ensure that neither level of government overreached its authority.

Our case was argued back-to-back with the Liberty University case, also against the mandate. I found two of the federal government's statements in that case to be particularly interesting.

The first statement described what the government intended to regulate with the individual mandate. The administration's lawyers said that the mandate was part of an attempt to "regulate the decision to self-insure" (that is, paying for your own health care expenses).

Remember that the Commerce Clause cases during the last one hundred years had all addressed Congress regulating some sort of *activity*. Putting the decision to *not* buy insurance in terms of "self-insuring" was the feds' way of trying to make an individual's decision not to participate in an activity actually look like it *was* an activity. Hey, "insuring" yourself (not really) was no different than buying insurance, so the government could regulate that, too.

They were really going all out again with the word games, and with each legal brief and court appearance, we were always fascinated to find out what new word twists they had come up with.

The feds went on to push the argument that a "decision" was equivalent to an "activity." In other words, thinking about not doing something was really doing something.

If you're having a hard time understanding this logic, that's probably because it's completely illogical.

But the government *did* get some federal judges to buy into it. A district court judge in one case in Washington, DC, agreed with this line of thinking and argued in her opinion that, yes, the government was actually regulating an activity—namely, "mental activity." You read that right: a federal judge ruled that your mental activity could be regulated by the federal government! If George Orwell were alive, he would be thinking he had plenty of material for a *1984* sequel!

The second statement the federal government made in the Fourth Circuit that was particularly interesting came at the end of more than two hours of argument. One of the judges indicated that she was not comfortable with how the federal government attempted to address the activity/inactivity distinction. In response, the lawyer for the government said that even if the court found that there was no activity of any kind, the law was constitutional *anyway*.

Think of how astonishing that statement was! Instead of trying to convince the court that their first argument was correct, the lawyers for the government finally broke down and said that they *didn't even need* any activity; they could just order you to buy health insurance. Up until that point, the federal lawyers had danced around that issue in every court appearance. But when pressed by a federal judge, they finally conceded the total sweeping nature of their claim of power.

The government was claiming it didn't need constitutional or legal authority to do something. It wanted to do whatever it wanted to do, and when challenged about it, the government finally just declared, "Because I said so." The nanny state was really living up to its nickname.

Four months later, on September 8, 2011, the Fourth Circuit handed down its decision. The court decided unanimously to throw out our case based on standing (saying we had no right to sue) without deciding the constitutional questions that were at the center of the suit. On the issue of standing, the court said that if Virginia were allowed to bring a lawsuit like this one, it could lead to the states' becoming "constitutional watchdogs" over the federal government.

What?!?

Hold on a minute! The states are *supposed* to be constitutional watchdogs over the federal government, just as the federal government is supposed to be a constitutional watchdog over the states. That was exactly how the Founding Fathers planned it. As that "radical" James Madison wrote in *Federalist No. 51*:

> In the compound republic of America, the power surrendered by the people is first divided between two distinct governments, and then the portion allotted to each subdivided among distinct and separate departments. Hence a double security arises to the rights of the people. *The different governments will control each other*, at the same time that each will be controlled by itself. [Emphasis added.]

Part of the founders' rationale in setting up the system of federal courts was so that the courts could referee exactly the kinds of disputes over the constitutional boundaries between the two levels of government that Virginia was contesting in the health care case.

The Fourth Circuit Court's reasoning was entirely at odds with America's constitutional design and a dismissal of the states' role in our federal form of government. No other federal appellate court at any time in American history had ever (yes, you read that right: *ever*) denied a state's standing to defend its own code of laws—in the health care case or in any other case. That kind of dismissal of a state's role in our constitutional system was simply unprecedented.

It was finally time to appeal to the Supreme Court.

CHAPTER 7

A SUPREME DEBATE

|||||||||||||||||||||||||||||||||||||||||||||||||||||||||||||||||||||||||||||||||||||||||||||||||||||||||||||||||||||

I offer nothing more than simple facts, plain arguments,
and common sense.

—THOMAS PAINE, American political theorist
who greatly influenced the American Revolution,
from his 1776 pamphlet, *Common Sense*

Health Care Reform Finally Makes It
to the U.S. Supreme Court

IN AUGUST 2011, the judges of the U.S. Court of Appeals for the Eleventh Circuit in Atlanta handed down their decision in the Florida multistate case. The judges agreed with the earlier decision of the Florida district court that the individual mandate was unconstitutional, but the Eleventh Circuit failed to strike down the rest of the law.

The court ruled that the individual mandate represented "a wholly novel and potentially unbounded assertion of congressional authority: the ability to compel Americans to purchase an expensive health insurance product they have elected not to buy." Yet another court saw the tremendous threat to liberty this law posed.

The federal government appealed the case, and in November 2011, the Supreme Court agreed to hear *U.S. Department of Health and Human Services v. Florida*. The Supreme Court scheduled the longest oral arguments in nearly fifty years for the case: five and a half hours over three days—March 26–28, 2012.

122

Usually Supreme Court cases get one hour of oral arguments. Five and a half hours of Supreme Court time over three days really blew away any claims that all these challenges to Obamacare were frivolous. *The Hill* congressional newspaper even commented: "That the high court would set aside so much time for the landmark case suggests that the justices certainly don't see the challenges as a waste of time."

Virginia's case was put on hold at the Supreme Court while the court heard Florida's case. Since our arguments over the constitutionality of the individual-insurance mandate and its lack of severability were being heard through the multistate case, the ruling in *Florida* would apply to our case as well.

During the Supreme Court hearings, my role became one of highlighting the legal arguments and the strategies of both sides for the media, as well as ensuring that we were keeping in the forefront the message of why the Constitution and the rule of law mattered so much in this case. With so much of the public paying attention to the case, win or lose at the Supreme Court, it was an important opportunity to educate those Virginians and Americans who still didn't understand that Obamacare wasn't a free gift, but rather a very real threat to their liberty.

We had arrived at the point where the constitutionality of the health insurance mandate would rest in the hands of only *five* people— five Supreme Court justices who would make up the majority opinion. Five justices were the fail-safe for the Constitution. And since the court had at least one swing vote, not even five justices were the fail-safe; it was expected that the outcome might rest on one vote.

How had things become so broken in America that the future of freedom for 311 million Americans could come down to the decision of *one* individual? What had failed so badly that we were at this point? The problem had been one of decades of deference by the courts— and indifference by the American people—to the expansion of government power in Washington. That expansion was made possible through the loose interpretation—or rewriting—of the Constitution, which allowed the legal boundaries set for government to be stretched beyond anything the founders would have ever imagined. With that situation as a foundation, when a group of congressmen and a president came to power who were willing to stretch the Constitution to its breaking point—masking their own lust for power with the false promise of giving Americans something for free while taking their liberty as payment—the result was this Obamacare showdown.

A few days before the Supreme Court hearings, the gravity of the situation was clear. The *Wall Street Journal*—not a media outlet known for sensational journalism—echoed what we had said from the beginning:

> Few legal cases in the modern era are as consequential, or as defining, as the challenges to the Patient Protection and Affordable Care Act that the Supreme Court hears beginning Monday. The powers that the Obama Administration is claiming change the structure of the American government as it has existed for 225 years. Thus has the health-care law provoked an unprecedented and unnecessary constitutional showdown that endangers individual liberty.

Before and in the two years after the federal health care law passed, poll after poll consistently showed that the majority of Americans opposed it. In fact, an ABC News/*Washington Post* poll in March 2012—just weeks before the Supreme Court was to hear the case—reaffirmed that a vast majority didn't want the health insurance mandate to survive:

> Two-thirds of Americans say the U.S. Supreme Court should throw out either the individual mandate in the

federal health care law or the law in its entirety, signaling the depth of public disagreement with that element of the Affordable Care Act.

This ABC News/*Washington Post* poll finds that Americans oppose the law overall by 52–41 percent. And 67 percent believe the high court should either ditch the law or at least the portion that requires nearly all Americans to have coverage.

Regardless of public sentiment, though, the court's decision was supposed to be made based on the rule of law and the Constitution, not on polls or protests. Otherwise, the Constitution was just a useless piece of parchment, and the country could just devolve into a place where majority rule—without a set of guiding principles and protections for rights—determined what was lawful and what wasn't.

Recall that majority rule was what my first debate opponent—Clinton solicitor general Walter Dellinger—said would be left to protect your rights if the individual mandate were found constitutional. That wasn't hyperbole; it was honesty.

Under majority rule, we might have the right to speak freely this week, but next week that right might be taken away because popular opinion changed. Under majority rule, we might live in a pure democracy, but we wouldn't necessarily live in freedom. We would live under a "tyranny of the majority," where instead of having unalienable, God-given rights, popular will would determine what we could and couldn't do.

No, polls, protests, and media stories shouldn't have had any effect on the justices and their decisions. Frankly, part of the problem with some previous Supreme Court rulings appeared to be that the justices may have been taking these other considerations into account. To maintain a system of government that secures our liberties and treats everyone equally under the law, we need judges who will do nothing but make their decisions based on the law as it was written and originally understood.

The Supreme Court Arguments

ON THE FIRST day of oral arguments on March 26, 2012, the Supreme Court heard arguments on the Tax Anti-Injunction Act (AIA) to determine whether the states and coplaintiff National Federation of Independent Business could even bring suit prior to the individual mandate's taking effect in 2014.

The AIA was enacted in 1867 to require any lawsuits that challenged federal tax laws to be heard only *after* the taxes were paid. An individual needed to pay a disputed tax first, then sue. The rationale was that it was important to keep the tax revenues flowing to keep the government working without lots of nuisance lawsuits getting in the way. On the relatively rare occasion when the federal government lost such a suit, it could pay back the taxes with interest.

Even if the court found that the AIA applied and the case was dismissed, it would have just meant that we all would have been back in court in 2015 after someone refused to pay the penalty, because 2015 would be the first time the mandate penalty would be due for not having had proper insurance in 2014. Can you imagine the destruction that would have been caused by three more years of uncertainty about whether or not the federal health care law was constitutional?

The states argued that the Anti-Injunction Act didn't apply for a couple of reasons: one, because the mandate penalty wasn't a tax, and the AIA applied to *taxes*, not penalties; and two, because the AIA applied to *individuals*, not states—so it didn't stop states from bringing suit before any penalty was paid.

Back in 2010, when the lawsuits were just beginning, the federal government had argued that the AIA barred any suits until 2015. But eventually, the federal lawyers changed their position to agree with the states that the AIA didn't apply in these cases because the mandate penalty *wasn't* a tax for purposes of the AIA.

On that first day in court, Justice Samuel Alito chastised the lawyer for the federal government, U.S. Solicitor General Donald Verrilli, noting that "today you are here telling us it's not a tax. But tomorrow you're going to come right back in here and tell us it is a tax. Which is it?"

Verrilli stumbled as he tried his best to argue both ways at the same time.

Justice Ruth Bader Ginsburg seemed just as uncomfortable with the government's argument. She said:

> The Tax Injunction Act does not apply to penalties that are designed to induce compliance with the law, rather than to raise revenue. And *this is not a revenue-raising measure* because, if it's successful, they—nobody will pay the penalty, and there will be no revenue to raise. [Emphasis added.]

For Justice Ginsburg, a "revenue-raising measure" was a tax. And she said, "[T]his is not a revenue-raising measure." This was precisely the argument we had made in the lower courts about why the government couldn't use the words *tax* and *penalty* interchangeably.

Many people draw strong conclusions about what a particular justice thinks based on the questions he or she asks during oral argument. Drawing conclusions from questions can be a very unreliable predictor, as justices may just be probing lawyers to test the justice's own—sometimes opposite—conclusions. However, flat-out statements of position are usually much more reliable. And in this case, on day one, Justice Ginsburg flatly stated, "[T]his is not a tax."

On the second day of hearings, when the court heard arguments about the mandate, Justice Ginsburg, who seemed friendly to many of the government's arguments, definitively restated her position that the mandate penalty was not a tax:

> A tax is to raise revenue, tax is a revenue-raising device, and the purpose of this exaction [the mandate penalty] is to get people into the health care risk pool before they need medical care. And so it will be successful, if it doesn't raise any revenue, if it gets people to buy the insurance, that's—that's what this penalty is—this penalty is designed to affect conduct. The conduct is buy health protection, buy health insurance before you have a need for medical care. That's what the penalty is designed to do, not to raise revenue.

Justice Ginsburg was not saying anything extraordinary. She was simply stating a generally accepted legal distinction that the lawyers for the federal government refused to accept.

Given the eventual outcome of the case, there was much less discussion of this "mandate is really a tax" topic than one would have expected. Even though it was the most important fallback argument in the federal government's case—basically, a lifeline to keep the mandate alive if the Supreme Court didn't buy its Commerce Clause argument—it seemed like it was going nowhere with the justices, just as it had gone nowhere with almost every lower-court judge who had heard it.

In my newsletter to my constituents after the hearing, I wrote, "No justice gave any particular indication that he or she was ready to defend the penalty-equals-a-tax position."

Yet ultimately, just a few months later, this is precisely how the mandate would survive.

The Battle over the Constitutionality
of the Individual Mandate

THE DISCUSSION ON the second day focused primarily on whether the government had the power under the Commerce Clause to mandate that people buy a private product—health insurance.

Justice Anthony Kennedy seemed to agree that the federal government wasn't regulating existing commerce, but instead was trying to force citizens into commerce so it could regulate them. He asked the solicitor general, "Can you create commerce in order to regulate it?" Later, Justice Kennedy insisted, "Here the government is saying that the federal government has a duty to tell the individual citizen that it must act, and that is different than what we have in previous cases, and *that changes the relationship of the federal government to the individual in a very fundamental way.*" [Emphasis added.]

Frankly, this was the consistency in Justice Kennedy's philosophy from prior cases that we had expected. This was a powerful statement that seemed to indicate he had serious problems with the individual mandate, and I took great comfort in that. I believe the "fundamental" change Justice Kennedy was concerned about was the shift toward more government control at the expense of citizens' liberty.

While many people felt that Justice Kennedy would be the swing vote between the conservative and liberal justices in the health care suit, we didn't think that would be the case.

His opinions in previous, similar cases were consistently protective of federalism—the balance of power between the state governments and the federal government. A win for the federal government in the health care case under the Commerce Clause power would have significantly shifted that power in the favor of the federal government. A win would have nearly completely gutted federalism as we had known it for the prior 224 years.

It was just an educated guess, but we felt that Justice Kennedy's strong belief in "structural federalism" would be on the side of the states, and it would soon turn out that we were right.

Eventually, Solicitor General Verrilli was directly confronted with the challenge of identifying some limiting constitutional principle to federal power if the mandate were in fact found constitutional. Remember, since the Rehnquist Court in the 1980s, the Supreme Court had always looked for some limit, some boundary when the government pushed for an expansion of the Commerce Clause.

Mr. Verrilli identified two circumstances that he said demonstrated the uniqueness of the health care market that would restrict federal mandates from spreading to the other areas of the economy. First, he said that health care was unique because someone without insurance could be hit unexpectedly with huge expenses they couldn't afford to pay; and second, if the person couldn't afford to pay them, those costs would be shifted to others.

This prompted one of the funniest lines of the three days of hearings when Justice Alito immediately leaned forward and asked, "What about burial costs?" It took a second for the question to sink in, at which point the courtroom burst out laughing. Justice Alito noted that burial costs were expensive and could hit someone unexpectedly, too. And he said that if he were too poor to pay for his own funeral costs, he'd still certainly be buried, and those costs would be shifted to others.

Boom.

In one short question, Justice Alito utterly decimated the "logic" of the federal government's explanation of the supposed "uniqueness" of the health care market that would "ensure" no other mandates would—or could—be directed toward any other part of the economy.

Justice Antonin Scalia came up with another nonunique argument when he commented, "Everybody has to buy food sooner or later, so you define the market as food. Therefore, everybody's in the market; therefore, you can make people buy broccoli."

Chief Justice John Roberts noted that the government was trying to solve the problems in the health care market by regulating health insurance, yet the health care and health insurance markets were two different industries. He asked, even if the health care market were unique, what would stop Congress from coming back later with some other mandate that it rationalized would help with the health care problem? If the court allowed the mandate to stand, "You'll just be back with something else that's unique" to mandate later, he told the government.

Justice Elena Kagan seemed to advance the government's notion that the mandate was just the ordinary regulation of a national health care market, and that since we were all in it, or would be in it, it was all just a question of timing—of when the federal government could apply its regulation. At several points, Justice Kagan seemed to try to "carry" Solicitor General Verrilli through his own argument, as he struggled to make useful points.

She and Justice Ginsburg repeatedly said that people who decided not to buy health insurance had an economic impact on an existing stream of economic activity. Justice Kagan said, "The aggregate of all these uninsured people are increasing the normal family premium, Congress says, by a thousand dollars a year. Those people are in commerce. They're making decisions."

In other words, by doing nothing, people who chose not to buy health insurance were allegedly causing economic hardship for other people, because those who bought insurance had to pay increased premiums to cover uninsured people who couldn't pay their medical bills.

I would remind you that a major part of this problem was caused by the federal government in the first place when it passed the Emergency Medical Treatment and Labor Act in 1986. The law requires any hospital that receives federal Medicare dollars (most hospitals) to screen anyone who walks in the door claiming they need treatment for an emergency condition. If the person is deemed to have an emergency condition, the law says the hospital—regardless of the person's ability to pay—is required to provide stabilizing treatment to ensure the condition doesn't get worse.

Now, while no one wants to see someone who's severely ill or injured left untreated, these emergency room treatments are generally some of the most expensive treatments one can receive. Hospitals can't stay open by giving medical care away, so they have to pass a lot of those expenses on to their paying patients. They do this by increasing prices for medical procedures and hospital care. Since insurance companies pay for most of those medical expenses (and therefore, most of those increases) and insurance companies can't stay in business if their costs increase and their premiums stay the same, they have to increase their premiums. So, it's not the government, it's not the hospitals, and it's not the insurance companies that pay for uninsured people, it's you and your employer who pay the health insurance premiums.

Justice Kagan was right—the aggregate effect of all the uninsured people using medical care they couldn't pay for was increasing insurance premiums. But the government had helped create this problem, and now it was trying to solve it with even more government. First it put a mandate on the hospitals; and when that got too expensive, it foisted a mandate on the people. When that new mandate ends up causing even more problems in the future, will the government keep passing mandates to solve each successive problem? Where will it end? When we aren't allowed to eat butter and sugar for fear we will get heart disease and diabetes (because we'll all have to pay for treating those diseases)? When we are only allowed to take public transportation because cars cause too many accidents (which will be deemed too costly for society to cover)? When . . .

You get the idea.

The Arguments About Medicaid Coercion

O N THE THIRD day of hearings, the court heard arguments regarding the severability of the individual mandate from the rest of the law if it were declared unconstitutional. The justices also heard the states' claim that PPACA's Medicaid expansion represented unconstitutional coercion of the states under the Constitution's spending power.

Remember that Obamacare greatly expanded the Medicaid program and those eligible for it. The states and the federal government already shared the cost of the program, but with the new law, the federal government had unilaterally created a huge expansion that would cost the states billions of dollars more per year to fund.

The states argued that because they were so heavily invested and had millions of people reliant on the Medicaid program, they were essentially forced or "coerced" to accept the massive expansion dictated by the federal government. If they didn't accept it, the government would cut off all their Medicaid funding, including the funding levels that existed before the expansion. The states didn't have the money to maintain their programs without federal funds, as they had all become too financially dependent over the forty-seven years since Medicaid began.

Some of the justices plainly suggested that as long as the states had the right to refuse the federal money, they were not being coerced. Others seemed to suggest that Congress was using its spending power to unconstitutionally force the states to do its will, given how dependent they had become on federal Medicaid dollars.

Chief Justice Roberts appeared critical of the states' position, noting that, to some extent, their reliance on Medicaid was a problem of their own making. He said:

> Well, why isn't that a consequence of how willing [the states] have been since the New Deal to take the Federal

government's money? And it seems to me that *they have compromised their status as independent sovereigns* because they are so dependent on what the federal government has done, they should not be surprised that the federal government having attached the—they tied the strings, they shouldn't be surprised if the federal government isn't going to start pulling them. [Emphasis added.]

That statement really stung because it was so true.

For me, one of the most significant comments on the Medicaid issue came from Justice Alito. While noting that the federal government might be correct in its argument, Justice Alito said that if Congress can condition the receipt of all federal funds on accepting all strings no matter what those strings are, "then there is nothing left of federalism." Also true.

Severability: If the Individual Mandate Is Struck Down, Can the Rest of the Law Stand?

THE SEVERABILITY ISSUE would only come into play if the court found the individual mandate or some other portion of the law unconstitutional.

Three basic positions were argued here. The states argued that the individual mandate was so central to the law that the whole law had to be struck down if the mandate were unconstitutional. The federal government argued that if the mandate were unconstitutional, the mandate and the other provisions that relied on it (insurance companies couldn't deny coverage for preexisting conditions, et cetera) must be struck down, but the rest of the law must stand. Finally, a lawyer appointed by the court to argue a third position argued that, if the mandate were unconstitutional, only the mandate should be struck down.

Justice Kagan noted that if the court found the mandate unconstitutional, but left in place the provision allowing preexisting conditions and other provisions that depended on the mandate, the whole health insurance system would be unsustainable. She said:

> Once you say that the insurance companies have to cover all of the sick people and all of the old people, the rates climb. More and more young people and healthy people say, why should we participate, we can just get it later when we get sick. So they leave the market, the rates go up further, more people leave the market, and the whole system crashes and burns, becomes unsustainable.

That was one of the few points she made with which I agreed.

All the justices concurred that the court must respect Congress's prerogative to be the sole lawmaker in our federal government, but their questions suggested two very different views of how best to do that. Some of the justices, particularly Justices Sotomayor and Ginsburg, seemed to suggest that the best way to show respect to Congress was to only strike limited portions of PPACA and nothing else. Others suggested that, to truly show deference to Congress, the court would need to strike the entire law, because to do otherwise would leave Congress with a law it never passed or even intended to pass.

Justice Kennedy said that if the court struck down the mandate but left the rest of the law standing, "we would have a new regime that Congress did not provide for, did not consider. That, it seems to me, can be argued at least to be a more extreme exercise of judicial power than . . . striking the whole."

Justice Scalia echoed this view, stating:

> My approach would say if you take the heart out of the statute, the statute's gone. That enables Congress . . . to

135

do what it wants. . . . It seems to me it reduces our options the most and increases Congress's the most. . . .

When have we ever really struck down what was the main purpose of the act and left the rest in effect?

All these questions would soon be answered by the end of June 2012.

After the Hearings

THE JUSTICES' COMMENTS and questions during cases don't often give a glimpse into the eventual rulings, yet many court observers and many in the media seemed to feel that the court was likely to divide along the expected ideological lines, with Justice Anthony Kennedy still a toss-up, but seemingly leaning toward invalidating at least the individual mandate.

The *Los Angeles Times* felt that the remarks of the conservative justices indicated the court "appeared ready to strike down . . . the entire law."

Mark Shields, analyzing the hearings on the *PBS NewsHour*, said, "And you could see this grow to the point where it's not only possible, it may be plausible that this law will be overturned, if not in entirety, in part."

I certainly felt better about the case after the hearings than I did before going in, but I've learned from a lot of experience that you can never judge how a case is going to turn out until the ruling comes down.

Meanwhile, sensing that they didn't quite have the slam dunk at the Supreme Court that they expected, many supporters of Obamacare went apoplectic—even the president himself.

From the very beginning of these cases on March 23, 2010, the professoriate, media, and political Left established completely unreasonable expectations regarding the outcome. They felt that anyone was simply ignorant for disagreeing with them on the policy or legal analysis of Obamacare. As one example, shortly after the hearings, I had a media appearance with Democrat attorney general Doug Gansler of Maryland. With a straight face, he declared, "This case should be 9–0."

Their reaction to the possibility of potentially losing was explosive and nasty. While taking the usual shots at those of us who led the efforts to defend the Constitution, they also turned viciously on their own. They criticized the government's lawyers mercilessly for their alleged poor legal performance at the Supreme Court, especially Solicitor General Donald Verrilli.

How bad was it? *Mother Jones* is one of the most reliably far-left publications out there, and here's what it had to say:

> Solicitor General Donald B. Verrilli Jr. should be grateful to the Supreme Court for refusing to allow cameras in the courtroom, because his defense of Obamacare on Tuesday may go down as one of the most spectacular flameouts in the history of the court. . . .
>
> If the law is upheld, it will be in spite of Verrilli's performance, not because of it.

But it wasn't just the left-leaning media that had picked a target. The week after oral arguments, the highest official in the land decided to weigh in, too. With two heads of state at his side in the White House garden—and on a world stage—President Barack Obama declared that it would be "judicial activism" if his signature piece of legislation were declared unconstitutional by the Supreme Court:

> Ultimately, I'm confident that the Supreme Court will not take what would be an unprecedented, extraordinary step of overturning a law that was passed by a strong

majority of a democratically elected Congress. And I'd just remind conservative commentators that for years what we've heard is, the biggest problem on the bench was judicial activism or a lack of judicial restraint—that an unelected group of people would somehow overturn a duly constituted and passed law. Well, this is a good example. And I'm pretty confident that this court will recognize that and not take that step.

The president's very public assertion that it was wrong or unusual for the court to strike down unconstitutional laws was woefully incorrect. Since its creation, the Supreme Court had struck down more than 160 laws passed by Congress as unconstitutional. As a former constitutional law professor, President Obama should have known that.

As the law that governs government, the Constitution put in place a system of checks and balances among the separate branches of the federal government that everyone, especially the president, should know and respect. Since *Marbury v. Madison* in 1803, the Supreme Court has served as a check on the other branches by engaging in judicial review—the process of determining whether laws are within the boundaries of the Constitution. Just as judges may not exceed their constitutional authority by legislating from the bench, they are duty bound to say no when the other branches violate the law or the Constitution. That's not judicial activism; that's an appropriate check on authority.

While ordinary, private litigants in lawsuits often complain that the legal system is biased against them or is somehow illegitimate when they lose, as a lawyer, I can tell you that it was wholly inappropriate for the president of the United States to engage in that kind of attack on the court while the case was still being considered. It was either an attempt to intimidate the court to decide the case in his favor or to delegitimize the court if the decision ended up coming down against him.

Of course, he was not alone. He was joined in his outrageous behavior by Senator Patrick Leahy, chairman of the Senate Judiciary Committee. In a May 2012 speech on the Senate floor, Senator Leahy directly addressed the chief justice, urging him to uphold the law:

> I trust that he will be a chief justice for all of us and that he has a strong institutional sense of the proper role of the judicial branch. . . . The conservative activism of recent years has not been good for the court. Given the ideological challenge to the Affordable Care Act and the extensive, supportive precedent, it would be extraordinary for the Supreme Court not to defer to Congress in this matter that so clearly affects interstate commerce.

CNN remarked, "It is unusual for a member of Congress to tell the high court how it should vote on a case during the weeks that the justices are crafting their opinion."

It was more than unusual. It was appalling.

All this is not to say the court is beyond legitimate criticism. But there's a proper time to question the merits of a decision, and that's *after* it has been rendered and you actually know the legal reasoning behind it. In fact, I'll be questioning the merits of the court's decision in the next chapter.

CHAPTER 8

WE WON . . . OR DID WE?

||||||||||||||||||||||||||||||||||||||||||||||||||||||||||||||||||||||||||||||||||||||||||||||||||||||||||||||||||

But a Constitution of Government once changed from Freedom,
can never be restored. Liberty, once lost, is lost forever.

—JOHN ADAMS, 1775

O N JUNE 28, 2012, the United States Supreme Court issued its ruling on the Patient Protection and Affordable Care Act. The states won three of their four arguments:

- The court agreed with the states that the mandate requiring all Americans to buy government-approved health insurance or pay a penalty was unconstitutional under the Constitution's Commerce Clause.
- The court also held that the mandate wasn't constitutional under the Necessary and Proper Clause either.
- The court agreed that the federal government's threat to withhold existing Medicaid dollars from states that chose not to participate in PPACA's new Medicaid expansion was unconstitutional under the Spending Clause of the Constitution.*

---

*The "spending clause" is really just the spending power under a broader clause of the Constitution that says, "The Congress shall have power to lay and collect taxes, duties, imposts and excises, to pay the debts and provide for the common defense and general welfare of the United States." The spending power is the part that says

140

With regard to Congress's Commerce Clause and Spending Clause powers, the Supreme Court expressly defined outer limits on federal power that hadn't existed since Franklin Roosevelt's New Deal.

If the Supreme Court had stopped there, liberty would have had a huge win.

But then, in a shocking move that few had expected, Chief Justice John Roberts joined with the four liberal justices—Ruth Bader Ginsburg, Stephen Breyer, Elena Kagan, and Sonia Sotomayor—to rule 5–4 to uphold PPACA's insurance mandate—not as a penalty under Congress's Commerce Clause power, but as a *tax* under its taxing power, which solely saved the mandate from being declared absolutely unconstitutional.

That meant that most of Obamacare and its mandate penalty (from that point forward, it would be called a "tax") lived on.

The court's decision saddled the country with a budget-busting health care law that would most assuredly increase health care costs and thrust a new $695 annual tax on the American people if they chose not to buy government-approved health insurance.

The Mandate Is a "Tax"?

MOMENTS AFTER THE court's ruling first came down, people thought the individual mandate had been struck down when Justices Roberts, Antonin Scalia, Clarence Thomas, Samuel Alito, and Anthony Kennedy said that it was unconstitutional for Congress to order people to buy private health insurance under the Commerce Clause. Fox News and CNN both initially had reported that the mandate had been entirely struck down.

"and provide for the . . . general welfare." But, for simplicity, I'll refer to it as the spending clause, because another part of the same clause, the taxing power, was also at issue in this case.

Chief Justice Roberts said, "Under the government's logic, that authorizes Congress to use its commerce power to compel citizens to act as the government would have them act." He was right . . . on that point.

But that was only the first part of Chief Justice Roberts's decision. He *then* joined the four liberal justices—Breyer, Ginsburg, Sotomayor, and Kagan—to say that the government could *tax* people for not buying health insurance. He wrote, "The federal government *does not* have the power to order people to buy health insurance. . . . The federal government *does* have the power to impose a tax on those *without* health insurance." [Emphasis added.]

So while the $695 penalty imposed for not buying health insurance would otherwise be unconstitutional, five justices said they would consider the penalty a tax, which would make it constitutional under Congress's authority to tax.

Both Democrat- and Republican-appointed judges in the lower courts had rejected that very tax argument on which Chief Justice Roberts and the other four justices were now relying. But calling the mandate penalty a tax was the only way the justices could "save" Obamacare. So they changed the name but left it functioning the same, and, in their eyes, that made it constitutional.

Justices Scalia, Thomas, Alito, and Kennedy issued a stinging joint dissent saying that the law should be stricken in its entirety. They accused their colleagues of "vast judicial overreaching" for trying to validate the mandate as a tax.

The chief justice wrote the court's opinion on the tax question and had to do two basic things to reach his conclusion: (1) he had to *rewrite* the Obamacare law to be a tax instead of a penalty, even though Congress had explicitly amended the bill to avoid calling it a tax; and (2) he had to expand the definition of a "tax" far beyond anything ever known before.

In the first regard, the conservative justices who refused to join Mr.

Roberts and the liberals said, "[T]o say that the individual mandate merely imposes a tax is not to interpret the statute, but to rewrite it.

"We have no doubt that Congress knew precisely what it was doing when it rejected an earlier version of this legislation that imposed a tax instead of a requirement-with-penalty. . . . Imposing a tax through judicial legislation inverts the constitutional scheme, and places the power to tax in the branch of government [the judiciary] least accountable to the citizenry," they wrote.

In regard to the second point, there are only four types of taxes the Constitution allows the federal government to assess: direct (or "capitation") taxes, excise taxes, trade tariffs, and income taxes. Direct taxes are assessed equally on everyone—they are per person (or "head") taxes and can be imposed on anyone merely because they are here in the country. Excise taxes are taxes on the sale of particular goods (for example, gasoline, alcohol, and cigarettes); tariffs are the same as excise taxes, except they are applied to goods imported into the country; and income taxes are taxes on earning income. The court majority who declared the penalty was a tax didn't say which one of these four categories of tax it fit into—perhaps because it didn't fit into any of the four categories.

In his opinion, Chief Justice Roberts didn't declare the mandate tax a capitation tax, but he tried to argue that it was *like* a capitation tax in the fact that no activity was required:

> First, and most importantly, it is abundantly clear the Constitution does not guarantee that individuals may avoid taxation through inactivity. A capitation, after all, is a tax that everyone must pay simply for existing, and capitations are expressly contemplated by the Constitution.

If it was *like* a capitation tax, but not one, then was it one of the other three allowed types of taxes?

Was it an excise tax? No; nothing was being purchased, so there was no opportunity for an excise tax. Was it a tariff on trade? No; nothing was being imported, so there was nothing to which to apply a tariff. Was it a tax on income? No; making an income was an activity, and again, the court said not buying insurance wasn't an activity.*

So it wasn't one of the other three types of allowable taxes. And it certainly couldn't be a capitation tax, because a capitation tax is a tax in which the same amount is assessed equally on every person in the country. The new mandate tax was not being assessed equally on everyone, just on those without insurance. Plus, the amount changed per person depending on how many people were in your household.

No matter how the justices tried to justify it, the mandate tax was still a "tax" on doing nothing—on not buying health insurance. The government was still using the taxing power (although we still didn't know under which kind of tax) to try to compel conduct.

Additionally, the justices had to ignore the court's own precedent that said a tax was really a penalty when its primary purpose became punishment for not doing something the government wanted you to do. Remember, in the 1931 *La Franca* case, the Supreme Court held that

> *if an exaction be clearly a penalty it cannot be converted into a tax by the simple expedient of calling it such.* That the exaction here in question is not a true tax, but a penalty involving the idea of punishment for infraction of the law is settled. [Emphasis added.]

The Supreme Court had previously said that Congress couldn't create such a tax for the primary purpose of getting around the Constitution to regulate something that it didn't explicitly have the consti-

---

*If a tax challenge ever arises, look for an attempt to say that because the qualification for the mandate/penalty is based on level of income, that it is somehow an income tax. It's dubious, but so was the outcome of the original health care case.

tutional authority to regulate. Unfortunately, that's precisely what this mandate-penalty-turned-tax did.

Now, while all the focus had been on Chief Justice Roberts's opinion, I want to give you a glimpse of another justice's opinion that didn't get any notice in the media: Justice Ginsburg's.

Justice Ginsburg remarked on both the first and second days of hearings back in March that, in her opinion, the mandate's penalty did *not* constitute a tax. In the last chapter, I mentioned that on the first day, while discussing whether the penalty was a tax in the context of the Anti-Injunction Act, Justice Ginsburg said:

> And *this is not a revenue-raising measure* because, if it's successful, they—nobody will pay the penalty, and there will be no revenue to raise. [Emphasis added.]

On the second day of arguments, Justice Ginsburg definitively restated her position:

> [A] *tax is a revenue-raising device*, and the purpose of this exaction is to get people into the health care risk pool before they need medical care. And so it will be successful, if it doesn't raise any revenue, if it gets people to buy the insurance, that's—that's what this penalty is—*this penalty is designed to affect conduct*. [Emphasis added.]

Obviously, given that Justice Ginsburg ultimately sided with the majority that ruled the mandate penalty was a tax after she had insisted it wasn't a tax during oral arguments, she appeared to have flipped her position. I can only think of two reasons for that: she changed her mind, or she abandoned her own legal conclusion because it was the only way to have the president's law upheld.

Given her clear and repeated statements of her tax position and the consistency of that position with the accepted legal distinctions between taxes and penalties, it appeared that Justice Ginsburg completely abandoned what she knew to be the constitutionally correct conclusion to get the outcome she wanted—to uphold Obamacare. A further indication that she likely abandoned her original conclusion is the fact that she didn't cite a single case in support of her new conclusion, nor did she explain her apparent reversal. She simply referred to the chief justice's opinion without saying any more on the tax issue.

The ruling that the mandate was a tax was unsupportable by any solid legal rationale or any intellectual history that traced itself back to the founding vision of our country, as evidenced by the fact that not a single brief filed with the court argued for the tax outcome.

Justices and judges are expected to practice the disinterested interpretation of the law, regardless of whether the outcome benefits or hurts Republicans, Democrats, or anyone else. This ruling was only the law of the land because five justices on the Supreme Court said it was. As citizens, we are entitled to expect more than what has been called "the rule of five" where the slimmest majority of the court imposes its rule without the ability to inspire conviction that the result is correct.

This ruling wasn't a failure of the Constitution; it was a failure of those who had sworn an oath to preserve it—from President Obama to members of Congress to the five justices who rewrote an unconstitutional law in order to uphold it.

There Were Limits: The Commerce Clause Can't Be Used to Regulate People Doing Nothing

WHILE THE COURT's decision on the mandate upheld a terrible law, other parts of the ruling did delineate some important limits to Congress's power.

In its decision, a majority on the court sided with the states on the Commerce Clause argument. The court said that the Commerce Clause only allowed Congress to regulate people who were *currently engaged in commercial activity.* It couldn't reach those who weren't engaged in commerce, even if they were *likely* to engage in commerce at some point in the future. In other words, the federal government couldn't force citizens to buy health insurance.

This was the court's clearest acknowledgment of actual constitutional limits on the federal government's commerce power since the New Deal. The court had adopted the activity/inactivity distinction that the opponents of PPACA had championed and that the big-government statists and commentators had ridiculed as being irrelevant.

Writing for a majority, Chief Justice Roberts recognized that

> People, for reasons of their own, often fail to do things that would be good for them or good for society. Those failures—joined with the similar failures of others—can readily have a substantial effect on interstate commerce. Under the Government's logic, that authorizes Congress to use its commerce power to compel citizens to act as the Government would have them act. That is not the country the Framers of our Constitution envisioned.
>
> The Framers gave Congress the power to *regulate* commerce, not to *compel* it, and for over 200 years, both our decisions and Congress's actions have reflected this understanding. There is no reason to depart from that understanding now. [Emphasis in the original.]

The most alarming aspect of the Commerce Clause portion of the ruling was that four justices (the four liberal justices) dissented and felt Congress should have the authority under the Commerce Clause to command American citizens to purchase private products, subject to few limits. Mostly those limits were when those commands directly contradicted the limited list of rights written into the Bill of Rights. Justice Ginsburg wrote:

A mandate to purchase a particular product would be unconstitutional if, for example, the edict impermissibly abridged the freedom of speech, interfered with the free exercise of religion, or infringed on a liberty interest protected by the Due Process Clause.

The four liberal justices also felt that "formalistic limits on Congress's commerce power," such as trying to distinguish between activity and inactivity and what had a direct versus indirect effect on interstate commerce proved to be a "nearly disastrous experiment" for the court during its history, and therefore should be avoided. So, if it's too difficult to delineate limits to Congress's power over the people, don't bother:

> It is not hard to show the difficulty courts (and Congress) would encounter in distinguishing statutes that regulate "activity" from those that regulate "inactivity." . . . Take this case as an example. An individual who opts not to purchase insurance from a private insurer can be seen as actively selecting another form of insurance: self-insurance [paying for his own health care costs out of pocket]. . . . The minimum coverage provision could therefore be described as regulating activists in the self-insurance market.

Those who doubt the importance of presidential elections and presidents' Supreme Court nominations should ponder carefully what Justice Ginsburg wrote in the dissent in which her three liberal colleagues joined. They wanted to uphold the law under the Commerce Clause, which would almost infinitely expand the powers of the government, but they were willing to join Chief Justice Roberts and settle for invoking the tax authority, if that were the only avenue available to avoid striking down Obamacare.

The Medicaid Expansion Was Coercive, So There *Was* a Limit to Congress's Spending Power

If Congress can do whatever in their discretion can be done by money, . . .
the Government is no longer a limited one possessing enumerated
powers, but an indefinite one subject to particular exceptions.

—JAMES MADISON, 1792

FOR THE FIRST time since the New Deal, the court also found a limit on Congress's spending power—a power many thought was virtually unlimited under the Constitution.

A 7–2 majority on the court blocked the federal government from withholding existing Medicaid dollars from the states if the states chose not to participate in PPACA's new, costly Medicaid expansion. Only Justices Ginsburg and Sotomayor dissented on this part of the ruling. The majority said:

> Nothing in our opinion precludes Congress from offering funds under the ACA to expand the availability of health care, and requiring that states accepting such funds comply with the conditions on their use. What Congress is not free to do is to penalize States that choose not to participate in that new program by taking away their existing Medicaid funding.

The justices felt the changes PPACA made to the existing Medicaid program were so broad that they essentially created a new program distinct from the one the states originally signed up for. They also said that, although Medicaid was a voluntary program for the states, the compulsion to accept the new expansion or lose *all* existing federal Medicaid dollars didn't give the states a meaningful choice about whether or not to participate.

Unfortunately, the ruling didn't spell out a clear test of when new federal requirements in future laws may cross that line. But at least for Obamacare's Medicaid expansion, the coercion was over. Each state could make its own choice of whether to accept or reject the expansion on its merits, without the threat of losing existing federal funding on which citizens had come to rely.

This part of the decision would save billions for the states that chose not to expand their Medicaid programs. Between 2012 and 2022, Virginia taxpayers alone will save around $2 billion if the commonwealth doesn't take on the expansion.

What Happened to Chief Justice Roberts?

IN THE PAST, Chief Justice Roberts had expressed the point of view that unelected judges had assumed too much power, and that courts generally should show more deference to those in the elected branches, who are closer to the people and can be voted out of office if the people don't like what they're doing. In his Obamacare opinion, he explained that he felt his decision was just the opposite of judicial overreach:

> The framers created a federal government of limited powers, and assigned to this Court the duty of enforcing those limits. The Court does so today. But the Court does not express any opinion on the wisdom of the Affordable Care Act. Under the Constitution, that judgment is reserved to the people.

He claimed that his decision to uphold the law was based on his deference to a coequal branch of government—Congress. He said he had "a general reticence to invalidate the acts of the nation's elected leaders" and that, if it were possible, he would find a way to rule the law constitutional.

Economist and Hoover Institution senior fellow Thomas Sowell said after the decision:

> [Chief Justice John Roberts] fell back on the longstanding principle of judicial interpretation that the courts should not declare a law unconstitutional if it can be reasonably read in a way that would make it constitutional, out of "deference" to the legislative branch of government.
>
> But this question, like so many questions in life, is a matter of degree. How far do you bend over backwards to avoid the obvious: that Obamacare was an unprecedented extension of federal power over the lives of 300 million Americans today and of generations yet unborn?

The *Wall Street Journal* was a bit harsher—though more in line with my view—in its commentary:

> [Chief Justice Roberts's] ruling, with its multiple contradictions and inconsistencies, reads as if it were written by someone affronted by the [federal] government's core constitutional claims but who wanted to uphold the law anyway to avoid political blowback and thus found a pretext for doing so in the taxing power.
>
> If this understanding is correct, then Chief Justice Roberts behaved like a politician, which is more corrosive to the rule of law and the Court's legitimacy than any abuse it would have taken from a ruling that President Obama disliked. . . . Judges are not supposed to invent political compromises.

On July 1, three days after the ruling, CBS News reporter Jan Crawford hit the airwaves with this bombshell headline: "Roberts switched views to uphold health care law." She cited "two sources with specific knowledge of the deliberations" for the information in her story.

She reported that Chief Justice Roberts was originally aligned with Justices Scalia, Kennedy, Thomas, and Alito to absolutely strike down the individual mandate but later changed his position and joined with the liberal justices to uphold it as a tax.

After he allegedly switched positions, the conservatives started a "month-long, desperate campaign to bring him back to his original position" that Justice Kennedy led. "In fact, Kennedy was the most forceful and engaged of all the conservatives in trying to persuade Roberts to stand firm to strike down the mandate. Two sources confirm that he didn't give up until the very end."

When the chief justice refused to come back to his original position, the conservatives refused to join any aspect of his opinion, including sections with which they agreed, the sources told her. In their joint dissent, the conservative justices "deliberately ignored Roberts' decision . . . as if they were no longer even willing to engage with him in debate."

This behavior is unheard of in the modern era of the Supreme Court.

Ms. Crawford reported that Justices Scalia, Alito, Thomas, and Kennedy believed that the mandate couldn't be severed from the rest of the law and that the entire law must be struck down.

Initially, when the chief justice was part of the majority that was going to strike down the mandate, Ms. Crawford reported that because he "was the most senior justice in the majority to strike down the mandate, he got to choose which justice would write the Court's historic decision. He kept it for himself." She continued:

Over the next six weeks, as Roberts began to craft the decision striking down the mandate, the external pressure began to grow. Roberts almost certainly was aware of it.

Some of the conservatives, such as Justice Clarence Thomas, deliberately avoid news articles on the Court when issues are pending (and avoid some publications altogether, such as *The New York Times*). They've explained that they don't want to be influenced by outside opinion.

But Roberts pays attention to media coverage. As Chief Justice, he is keenly aware of his leadership role on the Court, and he also is sensitive to how the Court is perceived by the public. There were countless news articles in May warning of damage to the Court—and to Roberts' reputation—if the Court were to strike down the mandate.

Ms. Crawford reported that the chief justice even tried to persuade Justice Kennedy and the others to join his decision "so the Court would appear more united in the case." Obviously, they didn't. Instead, *they* held their ground.

Did the Chief Justice succumb to the wholly inappropriate attack President Obama leveled at the court just a week after oral arguments in the case (and months before the decision came out), when the president said it would be "judicial activism" if the court declared his signature piece of legislation unconstitutional?

Unfortunately, whether the account is accurate or not, the possibility that Chief Justice Roberts flip-flopped to uphold PPACA will encourage future bullying by presidents.

Why? Because it looks as if it worked.

This apparent capitulation may have done irreparable harm to the perception of the Supreme Court's independent standing within our three-branch system of government.

After the Decision, Obama Argues, "It's Not a Tax"

EVEN BEFORE THE mandate was declared a tax, Obamacare already contained twenty new or higher taxes on American families and small businesses, according to an Americans for Tax Reform analysis of the law. These included:

- A new excise tax on medical device manufacturers (to be passed on to consumers and insurance companies in the form of higher device prices).
- A new excise tax on charitable hospitals that failed to meet new "community health assessment needs" and other new rules set by the Department of Health and Human Services.
- A new tax on employers with fifty or more employees that didn't offer government-approved health coverage at work.
- A new tax on income earned from stocks and mutual funds.
- A 10 percent excise tax on indoor tanning services.
- A new tax on health insurance companies (with the costs passed on to customers in the form of higher premiums).
- What I call a new 40 percent "jealousy tax" on expensive "first-class" health insurance plans. This tax is ironic because you are acting personally responsible—just as the government claims it wants—by buying health insurance to cover your family; but if you buy a nicer plan than the government *thinks* you should have, it will tax you mightily for it.

With all these taxes and plenty more already in Obamacare, I'm not quite sure what all the fuss was about trying to hide the health insurance mandate as a penalty.

All in all, the president's health care law was projected to cost $1.76 *trillion* over a decade, according to projections released in March 2012 by the nonpartisan Congressional Budget Office (CBO). As the *Washington Examiner* reported:

> Democrats employed many accounting tricks when they were pushing through the national health care legislation, the most egregious of which was to delay full implementation of the law until 2014, so it would appear cheaper under the CBO's standard ten-year budget window and, at least on paper, meet Obama's pledge that the legislation would cost "around $900 billion over 10 years." When the final CBO score came out before passage, critics noted that the true ten-year cost would be far higher than advertised once projections accounted for full implementation.
>
> Today, the CBO released new projections from 2013 extending through 2022, and the results are as critics expected: the ten-year cost of the law's core provisions to expand health insurance coverage has now ballooned to $1.76 trillion. That's because we now have estimates for Obamacare's first nine years of full implementation, rather than the mere six when it was signed into law.

After the Supreme Court declared the insurance mandate penalty a tax—*a tax that would hit more than just those families making $250,000 a year and up*—the president and the White House went into full-spin mode. They claimed that the penalty wasn't a tax—it was and always had been a penalty.

Remember, while campaigning in 2008, candidate Obama said, "If you are a family making less than $250,000 a year, you will not see your taxes go up."

How many times can you change your story in front of the American people until you lose all credibility? Apparently President Obama wanted to test that proposition out. In speeches to get the law passed, he said it wasn't a tax. On ABC's *This Week with George Stephanopoulos,* he said it wasn't a tax. Then while fighting lawsuits across the country in 2010 and 2011, his lawyers argued it *was* a tax. In 2012, in front of the United States Supreme Court and all of America, his solicitor general, Donald Verrilli, argued, "Not only is it fair to read this as an exercise to the tax power, but this court has got an obligation to construe it as an exercise of the tax power."

But then, when the Supreme Court let his law stand *only* because the justices ruled that the mandate penalty was a tax, President Obama and his surrogates claimed it was *never* a tax, but a penalty. From ABC News the day after the ruling:

> The White House and the Obama campaign today insisted that the individual mandate in the president's health care bill is a "penalty," not a tax, despite the Supreme Court's ruling to uphold the law under Congress' taxing power.
>
> "For those who can afford health insurance but choose to remain uninsured, forcing the rest of us to pay for their care, a penalty is administered as part of the Affordable Care Act," White House Press Secretary Jay Carney told reporters.

And when White House Chief of Staff Jack Lew went on *Fox News Sunday* three days after the ruling and was asked by host Chris Wallace about the court's ruling that the mandate was in fact a tax, this is the back-and-forth that ensued:

WALLACE: But according to the Supreme Court, this is
going to raise taxes for the families.

LEW: No, that is not what the Supreme Court said. What
the Supreme Court said was this was constitutional. They
said it didn't matter what Congress called it. . . .

WALLACE: Mr. Lew, they called it a tax.

LEW: No, actually, technically what they said is the Congress
has many powers. There is the Commerce Clause, there's
taxing powers, and it was constitutional. That's what they
said. It doesn't matter what they call it.

WALLACE: I can't let you go there. It specifically said that
it is not constitutional under the Commerce Clause;
they said it is constitutional under the tax. And as to
the question about raising taxes for the middle class, if
I may, sir, let's just look at the record. The nonpartisan
Congressional Budget Office estimates that in 2016, four
million Americans will pay the mandate penalty or tax;
75 percent of those people will make less than $120,000
a year. And the CBO says between 2012 and 2021, those
folks will pay $27 billion in additional taxes. . . .

LEW: I think if you look at all of the laws enacted in the last
three and a half years you would see that those families
have a tax cut. That say—all of the independent analysts,
whether it is the Congressional Budget Office or others,
would validate that there has been a tax cut for middle
class families.

WALLACE: I'm not arguing that. All I'm saying is that this is
a tax increase on the middle class of $27 billion over the
next 10 years.

LEW: No, what this is, this is a law that says if you can afford
insurance and you choose not to buy it and you choose to
have your health costs be a burden to others, you will pay

a penalty so that you will pay your fair share. That is what this law says.

A Fox News commentator aptly labeled the White House's reaction "a case of biting the hand that feeds" because the penalty-as-a-tax argument "alone spared President Obama's law."

Just two months after that interview, the Congressional Budget Office issued new estimates, stating that by 2016, *6 million* Americans (not 4 million) will pay the new mandate tax, and *80 percent* of those people (not the earlier 75 percent projection) will be in the middle class, making less than $120,000 a year for a family of four. The CBO estimated the mandate tax would average about $1,200 per household.

The one good thing about the mandate penalty's being called a tax was that Congress couldn't pull this same stunt again and try to get around publicly unpopular tax hikes by trying to force people to do something under the guise of the Commerce Clause instead of taxing them. Having to tax people and call it a tax would at least create some accountability and truth in labeling in the future.

Congress's political appetite to attempt things like this in the future will be limited—because these schemes will be, without question, tax increases. Is there any doubt that if PPACA had been presented as a middle-class tax increase instead of a phony guarantee of virtually free health insurance, it would have failed?

The States Still Had a Role to Play by Legally Refusing to Implement Parts of the Law

SHORTLY AFTER THE decision came down from the court, I briefed Virginia legislators about the choices they had on two PPACA issues: whether to participate in the new Medicaid expansion under the health care law, and whether Virginia should set up its own health insurance exchange through which people could buy subsidized health insurance or simply default to the federal exchange that would be set up automatically if Virginia didn't create its own.

These two decisions would be made by governors and legislators—not attorneys general, but my own position on both questions was that Virginia shouldn't proceed with either. Many other state attorneys general who had fought the federal health care law gave their states the same advice.

Although the figures I'll use below were specific to Virginia, the same basic concept applied to virtually every other state in the nation.

The proposed Obamacare expansion of Medicaid would have swelled Virginia's Medicaid rolls by about 40 percent, which would cost hundreds of millions of dollars more each year by 2019—an amount I considered unsustainable for the taxpayers. *And* that amount would continue to rise in 2020 and beyond. The states didn't have money just lying around to pay for these expenses. Where was that money supposed to come from? Were we going to take it from an already struggling transportation system? Or our educational system? Or were we going to burden more families with higher taxes? Even President Obama *used to* say that raising taxes in a struggling economy was a bad idea.

Looking back over time, we had seen Medicaid explode within the state budget—from about 5 percent to nearly 20 percent in 2012. And Virginia's experience was not unique. Medicaid costs had been overtaking the other parts of state budgets for years. Was this a part of the budget that we *really* wanted to voluntarily grow more?

But the feds were using a lot of bait to try and coax the states to undertake the new expansion. For the first three years, 2014–2016, the feds promised to cover 100 percent of the costs of providing Medicaid to the new additions. That would gradually reduce to 90 percent by 2022 and was supposed to stay at 90 percent thereafter. But even paying for only 10 percent of the expansion costs would *still* cost Virginia hundreds of millions more dollars a year—and that was an amount that was guaranteed to grow over time.

Let's also remember where these promises of all this money came from: the federal government, which was broker than broke. If the federal government were a person, he would have had an annual salary of $22,000, annual expenses of $38,000, and a credit card debt of about $162,000. Now, would you trust that guy to keep his word about paying back the money he owes you a few years from now? Add to that, the federal government was already borrowing from the Communist Chinese just to pay its bills. Where was this new federal money going to come from?

A simple truth is that math doesn't lie. Governors and state legislatures were likely to find themselves holding a lot of worthless IOUs for Obamacare funding when math finally caught up with the federal government.

Additionally, once states opted into the expansion, we would be at the mercy of the federal government. If we wanted to get out once we were in, we'd have to get permission from the feds. What do you suppose the odds of that would be? I likened this to the old Black Flag "Roach Motel" roach traps for the states: once you check in, you never check out.

But a more complicated question than the Medicaid expansion was whether Virginia and the other states should set up their own health insurance exchanges under Obamacare. You see, the health care law relied on states to set up these exchanges—government-run "marketplaces"—where people with no employer-based health insurance could go to shop for subsidized private insurance coverage.

PPACA called on each state to create its own exchange according to federal guidelines and to have it operational by January 1, 2014. If a state chose not to create an exchange, the federal government would step in and set one up for it.

Aside from the fact that exchanges were another added expense for states, Michael Cannon, the director of health policy studies at the libertarian think tank Cato Institute, shared with me an interesting legal objection to states' implementing exchanges—something many later called the Achilles' heel of Obamacare.

Michael put forward the idea that if states themselves didn't create these exchanges, Obamacare couldn't work. The reason was that PPACA stipulated that *only* state-created exchanges—not federally created exchanges—could distribute subsidized insurance.

Moreover, those insurance subsidies were paid for with the employer mandate tax (the $2,000 or $3,000 per employee tax for not offering government-approved "affordable" health benefits at the workplace) and the individual-insurance mandate tax (the $695 tax). Aecording to the law, it was the actual *payout* of a subsidy for the benefit of an employee that triggered the employer penalty and, for many individuals, the individual mandate penalty.

So,

. . . if the subsidies could only be paid out through a state-created exchange—not a federally created one,

. . . and a state chose *not* to establish an exchange,

. . . then the subsidies would never be paid out;

. . . and if it was the *payout* of these subsidies that triggered the mandate penalties,

then the penalties for employers and many individuals would never be triggered.

Wow.

So if Virginia and other states didn't set up insurance exchanges, their employers would default into the federal exchange, and the businesses would then have a defense against paying the stiff penalties. That meant that job creators could potentially avoid a huge new tax, and companies could instead invest that money to grow their businesses, give raises, hire new employees, and create needed jobs rather than turn that money over to the government.

Naturally, the Obama administration tried to counter this possibility by passing an Internal Revenue Service agency regulation that purported to "fix" the issue by allowing the IRS to extend these subsidies to the federal exchanges. The problem for the administration was that laws passed by Congress trump regulations passed by mere government agencies, so the existing text of PPACA would prevail. The only way it could be altered was if Congress itself decided to amend the law, and with the U.S. House in Republican hands, it looked as if that wasn't going to happen.

Michael Cannon wrote:

> [PPACA] provides tax credits and subsidies for the purchase of qualifying health insurance plans on state-run insurance exchanges. Contrary to expectations, many states are refusing or otherwise failing to create such exchanges. An Internal Revenue Service (IRS) rule purports to extend these tax credits and subsidies to the purchase of health insurance in federal exchanges created in states without exchanges of their own. This rule lacks statutory authority. The text, structure, and history of the Act show that tax credits and subsidies are not available in federally run exchanges. The IRS rule is contrary to congressional intent and cannot be justified on other legal grounds.

Defenders of Obamacare argued that, yes, laws do trump regulations, except when a law is unclear, and the regulation is meant to clarify it. The problem for them was that the law wasn't unclear on this point. The language exempting companies from the tax penalty in states that didn't set up their own exchanges was pretty indisputable.

Plus, on this issue, we already had a little help from the Supreme Court. In dealing with the severability question, the four dissenters in the health care ruling—Justices Scalia, Kennedy, Thomas, and Alito—wrote about this employer tax penalty provision and also found the language pretty clear:

> [T]he ACA makes a direct link between the employer-responsibility assessment and the exchanges. The financial assessment against employers occurs only under certain conditions. One of them is the purchase of insurance by an employee on an exchange. With no exchanges, there are no purchases on the exchanges; and with no purchases on the exchanges, there is nothing to trigger the employer-responsibility assessment.

With the IRS pushing its regulation in direct contradiction to the law as it was passed, it looked as if another legal showdown over Obamacare was inevitable.

As a Tax, at Least Repeal Was Within Reach

SINCE THE SUPREME Court reclassified Obamacare as a tax, it suddenly became easier to repeal. Unlike its original passage, which took 60 votes to overcome a filibuster in the U.S. Senate, a bill to repeal a tax is a revenue bill, which can't be filibustered. A repeal bill only needed a simple majority in the Senate—51, not 60, votes and a Republican president to sign it. The House had already passed a repeal bill in 2011, but the measure could never get enough votes in the Senate.

That made the November 2012 federal elections all the more important, as proponents for repeal tried to get their numbers to at least 51 in the Senate (or 50 plus Congressman Paul Ryan as the vice president to break a 50–50 tie).

It was certainly within reach to turn the Senate to a repeal majority in November 2012. In the November 2010 elections that followed the federal health care law's enactment, the Republican Party gained the largest number of seats in the House of Representatives since 1938. The 1938 elections were a rebuke to Democrats and President Franklin Roosevelt for Roosevelt's attempt to intimidate the Supreme Court justices who ruled against several of the big-government expansions of his New Deal legislation.

Unfortunately, in November 2012, President Obama won reelection and the Democrats retained control of the Senate. The chance for repeal was likely over.

There Was Always Value in Fighting

ALTHOUGH THE STATE attorneys general had won three of their four arguments, the federal government's ability to punish citizens for not buying health insurance was still upheld, albeit with a contrived legal fiction. The Supreme Court decision was painful for us and for America. But we had to keep fighting federal overreaches, because if there weren't enough lawmakers in Washington who were willing to uphold their oaths and adhere to the Constitution and the rule of law to stop the overreaches, state attorneys general—on behalf of the states—were the last line of defense for the Constitution.

Even the *New York Times* saw the validity of our challenge from the states, saying:

> Few handicappers gave a band of Republican attorneys general much chance of success when they filed a constitutional challenge to President Obama's health care law just minutes after it was signed on March 23, 2010. Some mocked them, while others largely ignored them. . . .
>
> While they fell short of their ultimate goal, they got

much farther than almost anyone had predicted, and can claim significant victories—both legal and political. The intellectual underpinning of the litigation had always been the argument that the health care law's individual-insurance mandate was an unconstitutional use of Congress's authority to regulate commerce. On that score, the attorneys general won.

Even After Repeal, Health Care Reform Will Still Be Needed

I F OBAMACARE IS someday repealed, Congress needs to come up with a replacement that addresses our real health care problems while getting government mostly out of the way. The more the government is involved, the further patients are removed from the decisions about their own health care and the less incentive they have to keep costs down.

Excessive government involvement has been one of the biggest causes of increased health insurance costs. True federal reform should give more power to the citizen-consumer instead of to the government and should bring to the consumer an awareness of the actual cost of care, which ultimately brings prices down through consumer choice and competition. Reforms should:

- Allow the purchase of insurance across state lines. It shouldn't be illegal for Virginia consumers to choose a Colorado policy if that policy has the coverage and price that best fits their needs.
- Encourage personal ownership of insurance policies by giving individuals who purchase their own insurance the same tax deduction employers get when they purchase insurance

for their employees. Such a deduction would reduce the out-of-pocket cost for premiums for individual policies and would reduce the problem of nonportability if one leaves an employer. It would also allow individual consumers to shop the marketplace for the amount and type of coverage they need and are willing to pay for.

- Incentivize the use of high-deductible health savings accounts (HSAs), which have lower premiums because they allow consumers to pay out of pocket for routine expenses while giving them insurance protection against more catastrophic costs. HSAs encourage individuals to monitor their health care costs, and they create incentives for individuals to use only those medical services they feel are necessary, which keeps premiums more affordable. If you aren't going to the doctor every time you have the sniffles because you have to pay $70 out of pocket for the visit instead of just a $20 co-pay, your insurance is going to be cheaper.

In addition, states should consider the following steps to reduce health care costs for consumers:

- Reduce the number of mandated benefits that state legislatures require insurers to cover in their policies. Mandates increase the cost of premiums dramatically. Why should consumers be forced to pay for four or five or ten extra benefits that they will likely never use? Instead, allow additional benefit packages to be offered in a menu as add-ons to a cost-efficient base package of benefits.
- Eliminate restrictions against purchasing health insurance across state lines. A small number of states have already begun this process.
* Require transparency in pricing, so apples-to-apples

comparisons among providers are easier for consumers to
evaluate. Just as you comparison-shop for groceries to find
cheaper prices or higher-quality products, you should be able
to do the same thing with medical services. This is a critical
element to rebuilding a market for health care services.

- Put caps on malpractice liability. The cost of the enormous
  premiums doctors pay for malpractice insurance ultimately is
  borne by consumers through higher health insurance premiums and the higher costs imposed by expensive defensive
  medicine practices. An example of defensive medicine is
  when the doctor orders ten obscure and expensive tests for
  you even though you only need one. He does that because
  he doesn't want to get sued if you find out later you were the
  one in a million people who needed test number nine and
  you didn't get it. So every patient gets all ten tests, which
  increases medical costs exponentially.

There are no silver bullets to making health care and health insurance affordable for everyone overnight, but an empowered, informed,
cost-conscious consumer who can choose among many competing
providers based on price and quality will encourage innovation, force
prices lower, and improve the efficiency of the entire system, leading
to increased access and better health care for all Americans.

CHAPTER 9

WEIRD SCIENCE

||||||||||||||||||||||||||||||||||||||||||||||||||||||||||||||||||||||||||||||||||||||||||||||||||||

The essence of Government is power; and power, lodged as it must be in human hands, will ever be liable to abuse.

—JAMES MADISON, 1829, Founding Father
and author of the Constitution

As BAD AS the federal health care law was, the draconian regulations that the Environmental Protection Agency had in store for the nation were almost as offensive to our freedom and our economy. The Environmental Protection Agency was another front in Virginia's federalism fight.

In 2009, when President Obama saw that even a Democrat-controlled Congress might have trouble passing a cap-and-trade law to force the first-ever limits on America's carbon dioxide emissions, he decided to have his EPA come up with its own version of cap-and-trade—one that didn't have to go through lawmakers to get approved.

The problem was, the EPA version was based on junk science borrowed from the United Nations, and the ensuing excessive regulations would eventually so tightly regulate the American economy that they were going to permanently push companies and jobs out of the United States; force people to drive less, heat and cool their homes less, and use their appliances less; and raise the cost of consumer goods and energy for the average family by thousands of dollars a year.

The other problem was, the EPA broke the law to give itself this vast and destructive new power. That's how I got involved.

What Was Cap-and-Trade, and Why Was It "Needed"?

SINCE THE 1980s, many climate scientists claimed the earth had warmed at a rapid pace during the last century because of a continuing buildup of gases created by human activity that trapped heat in the atmosphere, producing a "greenhouse effect." They claimed that the increasing heat from the greenhouse effect would melt glaciers and raise sea levels, destroy crops and starve the people and animals that depended on them, and make the air harder to breathe for all living creatures. There were six gases* identified as causing this greenhouse effect, and they were released by burning fossil fuels such as coal, oil, and natural gas, and through other human activity.

Cap-and-trade (derisively known as cap-and-tax, because that's what it really was) was a scheme Congress initially tried to pass under the guise of stopping global warming by capping the total amount of greenhouse gases that factories, automobiles, oil refineries, and power plants could emit into the atmosphere. Existing businesses would be given permits that would allow each one to emit a certain amount of carbon dioxide. If a business needed to emit more than the permit allowed, it could buy emissions credits from other companies that didn't use all of theirs.

Over time, the government planned to reduce the total allowable carbon emissions nationally to levels last seen 80 to 150 years ago, depending on which cap-and-trade plan you looked at. Currently, few

---

*The EPA's endangerment finding covered six greenhouse gases: carbon dioxide, methane, nitrous oxide, hydro fluorocarbons, per fluorocarbons, and sulfur hexafluoride.

technologies exist to help industries reduce emissions to those levels, and no one knows when or if the technologies will even be invented.

The EPA Announces a New Power: It Will Regulate Greenhouse Gas Emissions

JUST TO GIVE you a little history, in the 2007 Supreme Court case *Massachusetts v. Environmental Protection Agency,* twelve states brought suit against the EPA to force the agency to regulate carbon dioxide and other greenhouse gases as pollutants. The court ruled 5–4 in favor of the states, saying that the EPA was obligated under the Clean Air Act to regulate greenhouse gases *if* it ultimately determined they were pollutants that endangered public health.

In December 2009, in anticipation of Congress's inability to muster the votes to pass a cap-and-trade bill (the public was against it), the EPA issued an "endangerment finding," finally ruling that carbon dioxide and five other greenhouse gases were pollutants dangerous to public health because they allegedly caused global warming. This ruling gave the agency a broad new power to strictly regulate emissions in everything from factories to power plants to automobiles, essentially performing the same function as cap-and-trade legislation, but bypassing the people's elected representatives to do it.

The biggest target of the EPA was carbon dioxide.*

If the EPA moved forward with all the emissions regulations it was expected to propose, those regulations were projected to cost businesses billions of dollars a year in increased energy costs, fees for new EPA operating permits and construction permits for power plants and other emitters, costs to retool machinery to meet emissions standards,

---

*Since carbon dioxide was the biggest target, I'll use the terms "carbon dioxide" and "greenhouse gases" interchangeably in this chapter, unless a specific distinction between the two needs to be made.

or fines for not meeting the standards. Industries that couldn't afford these new costs or that weren't able to pass them on to their customers would be forced to close or move overseas where regulations weren't as strict, resulting in permanent job losses for Americans.

So, while President Obama's regulatory onslaught was killing jobs in America, it stood to become one of China's biggest employment programs.

Because businesses that remained in the United States passed on the increased cost of energy and regulatory compliance to their customers, virtually all costs for regulation would eventually filter down to the American consumer. The cost projections were thousands of dollars annually for every American household: the costs of electricity, gasoline, and heating oil would go up; and the costs for any goods that required energy to manufacture or transport would dramatically increase as well—food, cars, clothing, appliances, toys, lawn equipment, building supplies—virtually everything.

But this wasn't a problem for the Obama administration; this was exactly the plan. One of the stated purposes of a greenhouse gas reduction/cap-and-trade style scheme was to drive energy prices high enough to discourage consumers from using traditional energy sources. It was meant to get them to use less heat, use less air-conditioning, drive fewer miles, use less computing power, and use fewer lights. In essence, it would completely reverse the direction of the standard of living in the United States.

In an interview with the *San Francisco Chronicle* during his 2008 presidential campaign, Barack Obama said:

> Under my plan of a cap-and-trade system, electricity
> rates would necessarily skyrocket.

And what's worse was that the people who were hurt first and hurt worst as a result of these costly regulations were the poor. While big-government statists claimed to have so much compassion for the poor, they loved their intrusive and expensive regulations more. The poor were the ones who would disproportionately lose the manufacturing jobs when companies downsized, closed, or moved overseas; and the poor were the ones who could least afford the increased costs to heat their homes, fill up their cars, and put food on the table for their families.

One of the poorest parts of Virginia—in fact, one of the poorest parts of America, Appalachia—is where coal is mined. And coal is the main employer and economic engine in that part of Virginia. Unfortunately, coal was at the top of the EPA's hit list. During his 2008 campaign, President Obama even said he wanted to bankrupt the industry. The people of Appalachia were a prime example of those who would be hit doubly hard by these regulations.

But the EPA's supporters said the coal miners wouldn't miss their jobs because new jobs in the "green economy" would easily outnumber the jobs lost in the coal industry. However, in Spain, a country that President Obama held up as a shining example of a green-jobs-creating economy to emulate, quite the opposite happened. For every green job created, 2.2 other private-sector jobs were lost.

We really didn't have to look overseas for examples, though; the failures were already occurring right here at home. Several green energy companies in the United States required government subsidies to operate—meaning they weren't financially viable on their own. Even with the help of taxpayer money, several of them failed and went bankrupt. Solyndra was the most infamous example. Only two years after it received a legally questionable taxpayer loan for $527 million from the Obama administration to construct a manufacturing plant for its solar panels, it filed for Chapter 11 bankruptcy and laid off all its employees.

Even beyond the inevitable loss of jobs and the price increases lay another unsettling issue with the carbon dioxide regulatory regime: the federal government was going after America's energy supply.

While the country was working on finding alternative energy sources, the feds refused to face the reality that we weren't there yet: most of the energy that America used came from carbon dioxide–emitting fuels. According to federal data, in 2011, about *two-thirds* of the electricity that America used came from burning fossil fuels such as coal and natural gas.

We relied on that fossil fuel–based electricity daily to power our computers, our refrigerators, our lights, our televisions, all of our electronics, and even our electric cars! We relied on oil to heat our homes; power our cars; and power the transport trucks that brought the food to our grocery stores, the clothes to our department stores, and the packages we ordered off Amazon.com to our doors. Using greenhouse gas regulations to force Americans to replace these critical energy sources with more costly, less abundant, and technologically unproven and unreliable alternatives would undoubtedly slow the U.S. economy and potentially lead to energy shortages—with lines stretched around the block at gas stations, brownouts, and air-conditioning that wouldn't work on the hottest days of the year because of blackouts.

But the Obama administration didn't care about the economic consequences. In fact, the Obama-appointed EPA administrator, Lisa Jackson, said openly: "Economic consequences aren't my job."

Was Carbon Dioxide Really a Danger to Human Health?

BEFORE I GO on, I want to make one thing clear: As an attorney general, I was engaged in a legal battle with the EPA over the fact that it refused to follow the law when making rules the rest of us had to follow. But that didn't mean I was in a battle with environmental protection.

To the contrary, my office worked in close coordination with our Virginia regulatory agencies to enforce environmental laws. Several times during my term as attorney general, I also authorized my office to join the EPA in stormwater management enforcement cases against major homebuilders. I had even applauded the agency's efforts to punish those polluters while at the same time working out balanced settlements to achieve environmental compliance without hindering the ability of these companies to continue their needed work in my state.

My concern was that in making such huge financial sacrifices in terms of lost jobs, higher energy costs, and more expensive food and consumer products, we needed to make sure that the environmental regulations thrust on the country were based on the best science available; that for the incredible price we were paying, those regulations had a good chance of working; and most important for me, that the government was following the law and being fully transparent in the process. The problem was, in the field of global warming, it didn't look as if any of those conditions were even close to being met.

The EPA was attempting to transform the entire American economy and our standard of living because it said carbon dioxide was a pollutant dangerous to public health. Let's not confuse carbon dioxide with carbon *monoxide*, the odorless, poisonous gas that's also emitted during the combustion of some materials. No, carbon dioxide, or CO_2—this "dangerous" threat to America and to the world—is the gas we all exhale from our bodies every second of every day. It's also the gas that we readily and willingly consume when we have carbonated drinks. It's also what the trees and plants feed on so they can live and produce the oxygen we need *to breathe*. Yes, this important part of the "circle of life" is now suddenly a dangerous pollutant. Maybe it's worth keeping all of this in mind when we're trying to analyze problems carbon dioxide can cause.

In its zealous rush to create a new and unprecedented power for itself, the EPA took shortcuts around the law and didn't even take the time to perform the research it was required to do to determine if carbon dioxide was indeed a dangerous pollutant causing global warming.

Instead, the EPA primarily borrowed data from the United Nations' Intergovernmental Panel on Climate Change (IPCC). By (1) not independently generating its own data, and then by (2) relying on non-EPA research without even bothering to independently verify the data's quality, objectivity, and integrity according to required U.S. standards, the EPA violated the federal Clean Air Act, the Data Quality Act, and its own established procedures.

In its news release announcing the endangerment finding, the EPA claimed it had done a "thorough examination of the scientific evidence," which we knew wasn't true:

> After a thorough examination of the scientific evidence and careful consideration of public comments, the U.S. Environmental Protection Agency (EPA) announced today that greenhouse gases (GHGs) threaten the public health and welfare of the American people. . . . GHGs are the primary driver of climate change, which can lead to hotter, longer heat waves that threaten the health of the sick, poor or elderly; increases in ground-level ozone pollution linked to asthma and other respiratory illnesses; as well as other threats to the health and welfare of Americans.
>
> Scientific consensus shows that as a result of human activities, GHG concentrations in the atmosphere are at record high levels and data shows that the Earth has been warming over the past 100 years, with the steepest increase in warming in recent decades.

Failing to follow federal law was the first obvious legal problem with the EPA's endangerment finding.

The second legal problem with the endangerment finding was that before it was finalized, the Climategate scandal broke in November

2009, revealing new information that put the data the EPA relied on in serious doubt. E-mails leaked from the top global warming research center in the world—the Climatic Research Unit at the University of East Anglia in Great Britain—suggested that some of the world's most prominent climatologists had manipulated, overweighted, or hidden data to overstate the effects of carbon dioxide emissions on the environment to make it look certain that humans had caused the overwhelming proportion of any global warming. The UN's IPCC report relied on that questionable data, and the EPA relied on the questionable UN IPCC report.

In a situation like this, where relevant new evidence emerged that wasn't available during the public comment period, the federal Clean Air Act *required* the EPA to reopen its proceedings, to allow the public to comment on the new information, and to revisit its original analysis.

So on February 16, 2010, one month after being sworn into office, I petitioned the EPA to reopen its hearings on the endangerment finding and *follow the law* by independently verifying the questionable UN data it had used. We also asked the EPA to *follow the law* and consider the new contrary evidence from the Climategate scandal to see if it might cause the agency to reverse its ruling regulating carbon dioxide as a pollutant.

But violating the law yet again (once you start, it's hard to stop, and it can become a nasty habit), the agency refused to reopen its proceedings and consider the new information, and instead chose to unilaterally reaffirm in writing its prior conclusions.

It's worth noting that in rejecting the petition to reopen the public comment period to hear and consider new evidence, the EPA issued a *360-page document* explaining why it didn't need to reopen the proceedings. The agency took the time to write 360 pages of excuses that included over 50 *new* pieces of "evidence" to explain why it didn't need to consider any new evidence.

Did you follow that?

That just showed that the EPA had a specific end in mind and was going to stick to it no matter what. It didn't matter what the facts were; the EPA wanted to keep this massive control mechanism over the American economy, and nothing was going to stop it.

The EPA's refusal was a serious matter. It became obvious that it was exercising a political agenda, not a protecting-the-planet agenda, and the agency was willing to break the law to do it. Its push to reduce greenhouse gas emissions would soon prove to have a negligible effect on so-called manmade global warming, but the regulations it would develop would give it immense power over human activities that involved carbon dioxide emissions. From factories to cars, trucks, planes, power plants, office buildings, and even homes, the EPA could reach its regulatory hand virtually anywhere.

Virginia, Texas, Alabama, and eight other Republican and four Democrat state attorneys general* joined together in a bipartisan initiative to compel the EPA to follow the law in the largest appeal ever filed against a federal agency. Whatever the final decision on whether these gases should be regulated as pollutants that contribute to global warming, we all wanted that decision to be based on sound scientific data, not data that had been sifted through a political filter.

Just What Was Climategate?

IN NOVEMBER 2009, leaked internal e-mails and documents from the Climatic Research Unit (CRU) in Great Britain suggested that prominent climatologists questioned the reliability of their own data and the methods that were used to analyze that data. The e-mails showed that critical IPCC records were lost or destroyed; that scientists appeared to urge each other to present a "unified" view that

---

*Florida, Hawaii, Indiana, Kentucky, Louisiana, Mississippi, Nebraska, North Dakota, Oklahoma, South Carolina, South Dakota, and Utah.

global warming was manmade; that they may have manipulated their findings to overstate the effects of carbon dioxide on the environment; and that they also discussed ways to keep opposing views out of leading scientific journals and ways to keep skeptics from reviewing their data.

Phil Jones, the director of the Climatic Research Unit when the scandal broke, stated in one leaked e-mail that he was worried that fact checkers would try to get the center's data using British freedom of information laws, and that if he had to turn over his data, he said, "I think I'll delete the file rather than send to anyone. . . . We also have a data protection act, which I will hide behind."

Remember that these data were gathered using public funds, so they should have been publicly available. Additionally, sharing your data with other scientists to allow them to replicate your work is a basic tenet of the scientific method. It helps establish or undermine the validity of the science. If you don't make the data you used available, no one can go back and check your work. In the scientific community, that used to make your work suspect. At the CRU, and among many climate scientists, that was apparently standard operating procedure.

Many books and articles have been devoted to the debate over global warming, Climategate, and other climate scandals, so I'm not going to get into great detail here. I'm not a scientist, and our case against the EPA dealt with legal issues, not the science of global warming. I will only deal briefly here with some of the problems of climate science—not in an attempt to catalog every argument on either side of the issue, but merely in an attempt to give you a sense of some of the widely available information that created intense doubt about a "global scientific consensus" that humans were causing global warming. This was the other side of the issue that we cited in our lawsuit that the EPA never adequately considered when making its critical greenhouse gas endangerment decision.

Climate Science Is Exonerated? Really?

WHILE THE EPA and many media outlets frequently dismissed any problems with Climategate by pointing to inquiries by the British House of Commons, the University of East Anglia, and Penn State University that—they say—"exonerated" those involved in Climategate, the EPA and media outlets failed to point out that none of the inquiries addressed the *reliability of the data used* by the Climategate scientists, which was the central question in the states' suit against the EPA.

For example, the House of Commons Science and Technology Committee published a report on its inquiry but specifically declined to review the scientific validity of the climate data.

The University of East Anglia (UEA) examined a very limited selection of the work of its Climatic Research Unit. It only evaluated eleven articles, selected in part by Phil Jones, head of the CRU and a major target of the investigation. The UEA found merely that there was no scientific impropriety with only those eleven cherry-picked articles.

A separate UEA committee chaired by Sir Muir Russell, a former university administrator and chairman of the Judicial Appointments Board for Scotland, also reviewed the allegations made against the CRU. The committee didn't review the climate data either, but it did have a few interesting observations in its report. It suggested that the interaction between climate scientists and the IPCC had the potential to corrupt the science while misleading the public through the systematic suppression of how uncertain the science was. In other words, the only "scientific consensus" about manmade global warming seemed to be that it was really a consensus of uncertainty—uncertainty that was never shared with the public.

And finally, the Penn State inquiry never reviewed the climate data either.

Consistently enough, the EPA refused to meaningfully assess the climate data as well.

Climate Research: More Politically
Driven Than Scientifically Driven

MIKE HULME, A researcher and professor of climate change at the University of East Anglia, was one of the lead authors for one of the IPCC reports. He personally believes that climate science is and should be post-normal. What is post-normal science, or PNS? The creators of PNS described it this way:

> In the sorts of issue-driven science relating to the protection of health and the environment, typically facts are uncertain, values in dispute, stakes high, and decisions urgent. The traditional distinction between "hard," objective scientific facts and "soft," subjective value-judgments is now inverted. All too often, we must make hard policy decisions where our only scientific inputs are irremediably soft. The requirement for the "sound science" that is frequently invoked as necessary for rational policy decisions may effectively conceal value-loadings that determine research conclusions and policy recommendations. In these new circumstances, invoking "truth" as the goal of science is a distraction, or even a diversion from real tasks.

What does all that mean? It means that in their version of science, facts are uncertain, subjective value judgments take precedence over objective scientific facts, and scientific truth can be a distraction from the ultimate goal they're trying to achieve. So, creating the sense of impending catastrophe requires little more than alleging its possibility, not actually backing it up with science that withstands the scientific method. This is the exact *opposite* of the objective science that you learned about in school. Proponents of PNS have in fact admitted that it's more about achieving public policy goals than getting the science right. This meant that climate research was often more politically driven than scientifically driven.

Even renowned climate researcher and longtime advocate of the theory of manmade global warming, Judith Curry, chairman of Georgia Tech's School of Earth and Atmospheric Sciences, said in 2011 that there was no question that data from her fellow climate scientists in the IPCC reports were misleading and that "it is obvious that there has been deletion of adverse data" that would work against the theory of rapid global warming. "Not only is this misleading, but it is dishonest," she said.

And Professor Phil Jones, head of the CRU, admitted to the BBC in 2010 that he couldn't reproduce much of the temperature data he and his colleagues used to convince the world of impending global warming. These were the very data the EPA was relying on for its endangerment finding. This meant the EPA couldn't show the original data that backed up its finding, and that violated the legal standard for regulating under American law.

But what about all the global warming evidence presented in Al Gore's film, *An Inconvenient Truth*? In 2007, a British high court found the movie to be so politically biased and full of inaccuracies, it ruled that before showing it in schools, teachers were required to warn students with a disclaimer that it was a political work that promoted only one side of the argument. The film had been made part of the government school system's official curriculum.

Some of the major falsehoods the court identified in the film include the following:

- The film claimed that global warming was responsible for the disappearance of snow on top of Africa's Mount Kilimanjaro. The court found that no such link exists. A 2006 study concluded that the snow was likely melting because the glaciers appeared to be remnants of a prior period when the climate was able to sustain them.
- The film showed a polar bear desperately swimming while Al Gore narrated: "A new scientific study shows that for the first time they are finding polar bears that have actually drowned swimming long distances up to sixty miles to find the ice." The only scientific study the court found was one that indicated that four polar bears had drowned because of a storm.
- The film asserted that the rapid melting of ice from either West Antarctica or Greenland would raise sea levels by twenty feet or more. The court found that, according to the scientific consensus, if this happened, it would happen over hundreds—maybe thousands—of years, not any time in the immediate future.
- The film stated that low-lying Pacific islands are being flooded because of global warming, with Al Gore narrating, "That's why the citizens of these Pacific nations have all had to evacuate to New Zealand." The court found no evidence of any such evacuation.

Mr. Gore admitted in *Grist* magazine: "I believe it is appropriate to have an over-representation of factual presentations on how dangerous [global warming] is."

An "over-representation of factual presentations"? What does that mean? It's a convoluted way to say "exaggerating to the point of no longer being truthful."

As the British high court noted about the errors in Mr. Gore's film, they "do arise in the context of alarmism and exaggeration." That gives new meaning to "an inconvenient truth."

The point of all these examples is that the science wasn't "settled," more research needed to be done, and the EPA clearly had used data and claims that were in dispute, but it wasn't willing to look at any new data that conflicted with its original conclusion.

An EPA Insider Expressed Serious Doubt About the Data

BACK IN MARCH 2009, as the EPA was assembling the information to formulate its endangerment decision, senior research analyst Alan Carlin at the agency's National Center for Environmental Economics got an opportunity to look at the draft technical support document (TSD) the EPA had created to support its decision. He then quickly wrote a report to the people putting together the TSD, expressing his grave concerns about the information that was being used to make the endangerment decision. Following is an excerpt from his report's draft preface:

> We have become increasingly concerned that EPA and many other agencies and countries have paid too little attention to the science of global warming. EPA and others have tended to accept the findings reached by outside groups, particularly the IPCC and the CCSP [the U.S. Climate Change Science Program, which coordinated research on global warming by U.S. government agencies], as being correct without a careful and critical examination of their conclusions and documentation. If they should be found to be incorrect at a later date, however, and EPA is found not to have made a really careful review of them before reaching its decisions on

endangerment, it appears likely that it is EPA rather than these other groups that may be blamed for this error.

We do not maintain that we or anyone else have all the answers needed to take action now. Some of the conclusions reached in these comments may well be shown to be incorrect by future research. Our conclusions do represent the best science in the sense of most closely corresponding to available observations that we currently know of, however, and are sufficiently at variance with those of the IPCC, CCSP, and the Draft TSD that we believe they support our increasing concern that EPA has not critically reviewed the findings by these other groups.

Mr. Carlin's report then went on to point out readily available research that showed that global temperatures had been *declining* since 1998, while carbon dioxide levels in the atmosphere and carbon dioxide emissions had both *increased* during the same time period. That one piece of information alone should have been a red flag to the agency that the claims it was making were suspect.

The report also pointed out that new data indicated that ocean cycles and solar cycles were probably the most important factors in explaining the earth's temperature fluctuations, and that the "most reliable sets of global temperature data we have"—from satellite data since 1978—showed that changes in greenhouse gas concentrations appeared to have so little effect on global temperatures that it undercut the notion that greenhouse gases were causing global warming.

When Mr. Carlin tried to send his report to the team that was putting together the endangerment finding report, his boss wrote back in an e-mail:

The time for such discussion of fundamental issues has passed for this round. The administrator and the administration has decided to move forward on endangerment, and your comments do not help the legal or policy case for this decision. . . . I can only see one impact of your comments given where we are in the process, and that would be a very negative impact on our office.

Political columnist Michelle Malkin noted in her syndicated column that although the EPA tried to discredit Carlin, he had access to much of the same information the endangerment team did:

> The EPA now justifies the suppression of the study because economist Carlin (a 35-year veteran of the agency who also holds a B.S. in physics) "is an individual who is not a scientist." Neither is Al Gore. Nor is environmental czar Carol Browner. Nor is cap-and-trade shepherd Nancy Pelosi. Carlin's analysis incorporated peer-reviewed studies and, as he informed his colleagues, "significant new research" related to the proposed endangerment finding.

Although Mr. Carlin was not a research scientist or "climate scientist" any more than the EPA administrator making these claims or most of her staff working on them were, he was a senior research analyst trained in engineering and physics whose job was to review such documents. After tasking him for years to analyze these types of documents, the EPA couldn't suddenly claim he wasn't qualified to assess them.

Mr. Carlin could see that readily available data contradicted the data that the EPA was relying on, which again raised important questions about the validity of the information the EPA was using for such a critically important decision that would so dramatically affect the future of the American economy. He plainly admitted that he didn't have all the answers. The critical point here was, in the face of his laundry list of contrary data, his superiors preferred to suppress the information because it didn't "help the legal or policy case" for the endangerment decision.

Why Fudge the Science?

ONE REASON CLIMATE researchers may have given up the purity of science to forward a global warming agenda was simply for the research money. When researchers in the field of climatology predicted a global warming doomsday, governments were willing to shovel lots of money in their direction to try to find ways to stop it. The *Wall Street Journal* reported that the Climatic Research Unit at the University of East Anglia began to receive millions more in funding from the United Nations and world governments when the global warming hysteria began to take root with the public in the 1990s.

Then there were other scientists who probably weren't necessarily in it for nefarious reasons but who felt intimidated by their colleagues, the media, and high-ranking government officials around the world who insisted that climate science was "settled" and that anyone who didn't believe that was an ignorant "flat-earther" who would convict Galileo for heresy all over again. Remember that the e-mails leaked from the CRU showed that scientists frequently tried to stifle dissent and prevent dissenters from getting their work published in scientific journals.

The Hits We Were Taking

FOR OUR CHALLENGE to the EPA, several in the global warming–sympathetic media bombarded me with accusations of being against environmental protection. To the contrary, if they had looked at my record, they would have seen that my office worked in close co-ordination with Virginia's regulatory agencies to enforce environmental laws. I also have seven children who will be living on this earth for the better part of this century, and I certainly have a vested interest in seeing that they have clean air to breathe, clean water to drink, and unpolluted land to live on.

I was not suggesting that we go out and pollute the environment or allow individuals or corporations to freely dump toxins into our ground, air, and waterways. That should be—and is—regulated. But you can take anything too far, and doing "anything" in the name of global warming without good data and without regard to its financial costs and its cost to personal liberty was extremism. The EPA openly admitted it had no idea of these costs, so how could it properly weigh them against the perceived benefits of the regulations?

Additionally, because I requested the EPA actually support its research with credible data, I was also accused of being antiscience, which surprises me, as science is—or at least used to be—all about the data. I was a big proponent of data! As a former engineer (I was one before I became an attorney), I have a great respect for science: the scientific method, the certainties of the laws of physics, and the *objective* quest for truth.

I wasn't arguing whether global warming existed. What I was saying was that there was plenty of doubt that the science was "settled," which was the mantra that most warming alarmists pushed. And when the science was tainted by politics and money, and facts got ignored or hidden in the name of advancing a political agenda, it was no longer science—well, maybe political science. And when laws were broken in the process and states were told to merely step aside and accept it, that was when state attorneys general were in a position to stand up for the law.

My critics said I had a lawsuit against protecting the planet. They seemed to prefer allowing the federal government to break the law, but probably only as long as they agreed with the outcome. Regardless of whether the EPA regulations would protect the planet in a substantive way or not, ignoring the law to expedite a regulatory regime set a liberty-threatening precedent that we state attorneys general, who took oaths to defend the law, were unwilling to accept.

Democrats in Virginia charged that our legal action would cost too much money. I countered with the argument that the destruction of jobs and the increased prices for everything from energy to groceries would cost Virginians much more than any court proceedings with the EPA.

And frankly, if the EPA had simply reopened the public record on the endangerment finding, there likely wouldn't have been a need to pursue a resolution in court. Perhaps the legislators who were concerned about the costs should have joined with me and appealed to the EPA to reopen the record, as it should have done in the first place.

EPA's Own Analysis Shows Restrictions
Will Have Little Effect

THE EPA's OWN published analysis of some of its regulations demonstrated the questionable benefit of rules crafted from suspect data. For instance, I looked at the agency's 2010 proposed rules to limit the greenhouse gas emissions of cars and light trucks. The agency said the proposed CO_2-limiting rules would add about $950 to the price of each new vehicle. But buried deep in the proposal, the EPA's own models showed that for that extra $950, the regulations would only reduce global temperatures by less than three one-hundredths of a degree Fahrenheit (0.03 of a degree) *over the next ninety years* (assuming, of course, that the science is even correct)! In other words, we were going to charge people almost $1,000 to fit every new car with global warming controls that would do virtually nothing to stop global warming.

Despite this tenuous benefit, EPA head Lisa Jackson stated the results were so immense that they were "immeasurable." Well, she almost had it right . . . it was more like "unmeasurable."

And while it was thought that greenhouse gas reduction schemes in the United States would have a negligible effect on global temperature reduction over the next ninety years, China, which emits more carbon than the United States, was increasing its carbon emissions at a much faster rate than America was, and it had no intention of cutting back. The same applied to India and other fast-developing nations. They were looking for cheap, abundant energy sources, and fossil fuels fit that bill. They were even buying coal from the United States, all while we tied our economic hands with government diktats on every sector of our economy.

Did the Effectiveness of the Regulations Really Matter, or Was It the Punishment That the EPA Was More Interested In?

As I just pointed out, the ultimate effectiveness of EPA's regulations didn't seem to matter much to the agency. What seemed to matter more was severely restricting or shutting down America's fuel producers and the businesses that depended on them. The Obama administration and its EPA administrator didn't try to conceal their disdain for fossil fuels.

Recall that EPA administrator Lisa Jackson said that worrying about the economic consequences of EPA regulations wasn't her job. She didn't care if the regulations shut down businesses, destroyed jobs, or cost families thousands of dollars a year in increased prices for food and fuel.

And who could forget Barack Obama's promise to bankrupt the coal industry in an interview with the *San Francisco Chronicle* during his 2008 presidential campaign? Although coal was the single largest fuel used to create the nation's electricity (42 percent in 2011), Mr. Obama said:

> What I've said is that we would put a cap-and-trade system in place that is as aggressive, if not more aggressive, than anybody else's out there. . . .
>
> So if someone wants to build a coal-powered plant, they can. It's just that it will bankrupt them because they're going to be charged a huge sum for all that greenhouse gas that's being emitted.

For the icing on the cake, in April 2012, a video surfaced of top EPA official Al Armendariz, administrator of the five-state region including Texas, New Mexico, Oklahoma, Arkansas, and Louisiana. In the video, recorded at a 2010 speech the Obama appointee gave, he admitted that his general philosophy at EPA was to "crucify" and "make examples" of oil and gas companies, just as the Romans crucified random citizens in areas they conquered to ensure obedience to their rule. In the video, administrator Armendariz says:

> I was in a meeting once and I gave an analogy to my staff about my philosophy of enforcement, and I think it was probably a little crude and maybe not appropriate for the meeting, but I'll go ahead and tell you what I said. It was kind of like how the Romans used to, you know, conquer villages in the Mediterranean. They'd go into a little Turkish town somewhere, they'd find the first five guys

190

they saw and they'd crucify them. Then, you know, that town was really easy to manage for the next few years . . . there is a deterrent effect there.

A *Forbes* article published shortly after the Armendariz video surfaced said that he not only touted "crucifying" oil and gas companies, he tried it:

In 2010 his office targeted Range Resources, a Fort Worth–based driller. . . . Armendariz's office declared in an emergency order that Range's drilling activity had contaminated groundwater in Parker County, Texas. Armendariz's office insisted that Range's hydraulic fracking activity [fracturing the underground shale to let natural gas deposits escape to be harvested] had caused the pollution and ordered Range to remediate the water. . . . Range insisted from the beginning that there was no substance to the allegations.

Nevermind that he couldn't prove jack against Range. For a year and a half EPA bickered over the issue, both with Range and with the Texas Railroad Commission, which regulates oil and gas drilling and did its own scientific study of Range's wells and found no evidence that they polluted anything. In recent months a federal judge slapped the EPA, decreeing that the agency was required to actually do some scientific investigation of wells before penalizing the companies that drilled them. Finally in March the EPA withdrew its emergency order and a federal court dismissed the EPA's case.

So even though the EPA had *no* evidence that Range had polluted local water wells, it issued an emergency order giving the company forty-eight hours to begin supplying water to county residents and to start cleaning up the wells. And it took nearly a year and a half to finally get EPA's boot off the company's throat.

The EPA's Own Internal Investigation
Showed It Violated the Law

AN INCREDIBLE REVELATION came out in September 2011 in support of our legal position on the endangerment issue when an internal investigation by the EPA's *own* inspector general concluded what we had been saying all along: the EPA had failed to comply with the law and failed to review the accuracy of the data it used to conclude that greenhouse gases were a threat to human health.

Specifically, the inspector general concluded, among a number of other things, that:

- Rather than performing its own research, the EPA accepted work done by others, including the UN's Intergovernmental Panel on Climate Change (IPCC), and the agency failed in its "responsibility to determine whether the data met EPA's information quality guidelines before disseminating the information." This was a key component of Virginia's complaint.
- The EPA "did not certify that the supporting technical information was peer reviewed in accordance with EPA's peer review policy."
- The EPA's own peer review panel "did not meet the independence requirements" because one of the panelists was an EPA employee and the results of the panel's review were never made public, as required by law.

From the time Virginia filed its challenge to the EPA's endangerment finding in February 2010, we had stressed that our challenge was a legal one—designed to demonstrate that the regulations the EPA was attempting to force upon the country were the result of shortcutting proper procedures and federal law to push its agenda and vastly expand its regulatory authority over the American people.

These data quality and integrity rules were put in place to guarantee that the regulatory process was not hijacked by a political agenda—by either party. Scientists and government officials should operate in transparent ways, and the rules that the EPA failed to follow were designed to guarantee that transparency and to make certain that its conclusions were sound and based on the best available scientific data.

True science is testable, and true scientists willingly show their work and allow others to test their data, hypotheses, and conclusions. Whenever a government agency states a conclusion that is allegedly based on science, but refuses to comply with its own rules that require it to "show its work," we should all be concerned.

Yet in a statement issued two days after the inspector general's report, the inspector general stated that the "EPA disagreed with our conclusions and did not agree to take any corrective actions in response to this report."

No corrective actions? Again, the lawless EPA was moving forward with its regulation no matter what the law said and no matter who called the agency out on it.

A Federal Court Hears the Case

IT'S ALWAYS HARD to beat an agency in court because they get such tremendous deference by judges. Federal agencies are generally presumed to be right in most regulatory matters, which is a huge burden to overcome. We knew that going in, so we never had high expectations.

Finally, in February 2012, two years after we filed our greenhouse gases appeal, a three-judge panel of the U.S. Court of Appeals for the District of Columbia Circuit heard the fifteen-state case.

Four months later in June, the court rejected all arguments from all plaintiffs.

On the EPA's reliance on reports from the UN rather than doing its own research, or at least scientifically verifying the research that it borrowed, the court said, "EPA is not required to re-prove the existence of the atom every time it approaches a scientific question." The court said the EPA's finding that human activity increases greenhouse gases and contributes to global warming was supported by evidence. "The existence of some uncertainty does not, without more, warrant invalidation of an endangerment finding," the court wrote.

The court also said that the many challenges to the EPA's regulations were precluded by the 2007 Supreme Court ruling in *Massachusetts v. Environmental Protection Agency*, which affirmed the EPA's authority to regulate greenhouse gases.

Remember, in that 2007 ruling, the court said the EPA was obligated under the Clean Air Act to regulate greenhouse gases if it ultimately determined they met the legal standard to be declared pollutants. However, I don't believe the Supreme Court intended to compel such a destructive interpretation of the Clean Air Act as the EPA had taken with its regulations.

The circuit court at the same time acknowledged that the EPA didn't even take into consideration the benefits of activities that required greenhouse gas emissions (like driving your car or having electricity in your home) that would be affected by its regulations. It also acknowledged that the EPA didn't take into account how well the regulations it imposed would mitigate global warming.

The court said it would allow the EPA to move forward with regulations "even if the degree of regulation triggered might at a later stage be characterized as 'absurd.' "

The court also upheld the EPA's use of United Nations–generated climate data because it interpreted the Clean Air Act as permitting regulation even where "the relevant evidence is 'difficult to come by, uncertain, or conflicting because it is on the frontiers of scientific knowledge.'"

Wow, those last several parts didn't sound like a ringing endorsement of the EPA's work. The court seemed to have a split personality in its decision, sometimes chastising us for even bringing the suit, and at other times, pointing out how absurd and ineffective the EPA regulations might be.

Ultimately, we feel that the U.S. Supreme Court needs to clarify how far it will let the EPA take its 2007 decision, so Virginia and several of the plaintiffs will ultimately be taking the appeal to the Supreme Court.

I can only hope the Supreme Court will agree with the states and will conclude the EPA doesn't have the authority to make "absurd" economy- and lifestyle-altering regulations using "uncertain" or "conflicting" evidence without regard for their effects on the American people, their liberty, and their economic security. While the big-government statists declared the court's decision in this round a victory, handing over that kind of immense power to an unelected federal bureaucracy willing to shortcut its own rules and work under a veil of secrecy was a defeat for all Americans, regardless of their political persuasion.

From the beginning, all we asked the EPA to do was follow the law and reopen its hearings to review the conflicting data, as well as verify the data it had already used, so we could have an honest look at the information utilized to make such a massive command decision for this country. We continued our challenge in court because the EPA refused to do even that.

Co$_2$ws—Would Beef Be the Next
Thing to Be Regulated?

SINCE THE EPA had borrowed heavily from the United Nations to make its regulatory decisions, I wondered if it would also borrow data from a 2006 United Nations' report that concluded that the largest emitter of greenhouse gases wasn't even industry or the automobile (although, that's what most people were led to believe, since those were two big targets).

No, the largest emitter of greenhouse gases was . . . *livestock*. The gas emitted from livestock raised for human consumption, plus the energy used in the production of food for the livestock and the clearing of land for its grazing, caused more carbon dioxide than all the planes, trains, and automobiles on the planet—*combined*. At least that was according to the UN, so who knows how true it really is.

Did that mean the EPA would eventually put a climate tax on livestock, too? Would it attempt to tax chicken, beef, milk, eggs, cheese, and butter to discourage our consumption of basic foods (and foist yet another regressive tax on the poor), just as it taxed energy to discourage our use of it? Only time and the limits of the imaginations of unchecked, power-hungry bureaucrats like Al Armendariz will tell.

CHAPTER 10

POLLUTED THINKING AND
OTHER BATTLES

||||||||||||||||||||||||||||||||||||||||||||||||||||||||||||||||||||||||||||||||||||||||||||||

The true danger is when liberty is nibbled
away, for expedients, and by parts.

—EDMUND BURKE, 1777, eighteenth-century political
philosopher and founder of modern-traditionalist conservatism

UNFORTUNATELY, OUR BATTLES against an overreaching federal government didn't end with health care or just one EPA lawsuit. The Obama administration's absolute disdain for the Constitution, for laws it found inconvenient, for the role of the states in our federal system, and for the courts gave rise to my description of the administration as "the biggest set of lawbreakers in America." When the law, the Constitution, or the courts got in the way, the administration thought nothing of just ignoring them.

If you find that hard to believe, read on . . .

The Office of Surface Mining Usurps the
States' Authority over the Coal Industry

THE ASSAULT ON the states continued, and so did our commitment to pushing back. In 2011, the Obama administration ignored the law *again* to launch another attack on the coal industry

197

and challenge the authority of the states at the same time. This time, the administration used a little-known agency, the Office of Surface Mining Reclamation and Enforcement (OSM), to attempt to create more barriers to coal mining. The OSM came up with new, aggressive directives that went beyond its authority and allowed it to interfere with—well, more like veto—the states' issuance of coal mining permits. It also attempted to do its own rogue inspections of mines that were under the jurisdiction of the states. It was another effort to bring to fruition the president's promise to his environmentalist supporters that he would gladly destroy an American industry that they absolutely despised.

Under the Surface Mining Control and Reclamation Act (SMCRA, affectionately referred to as "smack-ra"), Congress gave the states the primary responsibility to permit and regulate surface coal mining within their own borders. Congress told OSM to simply review the states' general oversight plans from time to time to confirm that the programs were being correctly implemented. It did not give OSM the ability to deny coal mining permits, which it suddenly attempted to do in 2011. The problem with OSM's attack was that expanding the regulatory role of an agency was supposed to require Congress to pass a new law, not unelected bureaucrats to figure out new ways to increase their own power. This unlawful expansion of power had the backing of President Obama but flew in the face of a law that had guided the agency and the states for more than three decades.

OSM's newfound aggressiveness wasn't justified by any deficiencies on the part of the states in regulating their mining industries. It was because fossil fuels were cast as environmental villains and the Obama administration wanted increased scrutiny of mining permits issued by state regulators as a pretext to shut down coal. Hence the OSM unilaterally changed its role from one of oversight to that of a regulator and assumed the authority to overrule state regulators' decisions and interfere with states' issuance of coal mining permits. The

OSM also started conducting its own independent federal inspections of coal mines, even though inspections were the exclusive jurisdiction of the states.

Essentially, the president used yet another arm of the federal bureaucracy to attempt to go around Congress and go around states like Virginia, Kentucky, and West Virginia to attack fossil fuel producers and stop them any way he could. If Congress were too slow to pass a law or the president couldn't get his way in Congress, he likely thought the states would be easier to roll over.

But OSM simply didn't have veto power over states. If the agency were allowed to move forward without a challenge, the job losses in the poorest parts of the coal states would have been enormous. And with a country already too dependent on foreign energy, it didn't make sense to be so anxious to give up such an abundant source of *domestic* energy.

Burning coal was responsible for producing almost half of the nation's electricity. Coal provided more electricity to the nation than any other single fuel we had. The federal government aggressively tried to put whole industries out of business that didn't fit its green agenda, but it had nothing ready to replace them with. Green energy technologies weren't yet available to take coal's place. How were we going to create more electricity? Were we prepared for daily brownouts and blackouts due to electricity shortages? Did the president and his agencies just expect that we'd enjoy reverting back to an 1850s lifestyle?

I issued a cease-and-desist letter—a "nastygram"—to the Office of Surface Mining for its breach of the law, calling on the federal government to stop interfering with states' efforts to regulate mining, and threatening to take whatever steps were necessary, including litigation, if the agency persisted in overstepping the limited role Congress had created for it.

We were fortunate. This time, the agency backed off. We just didn't know for how long.

National Labor Relations Board Intimidates States
That Aren't Considered "Union-Friendly"

ON ANOTHER FRONT, in 2011, the National Labor Relations Board (NLRB)—a highly politicized, union-favoring federal board of presidential appointees—sanctioned the Boeing Company for building a new plane assembly plant in the right-to-work state of South Carolina instead of expanding its unionized plant in union-friendly Washington State. In South Carolina, because of right-to-work laws, employees were free to choose whether or not they joined the labor union at the Boeing plant. In Washington, state law allowed unions to require workers to join them as a condition of employment with the company.

The NLRB sanction was an unprecedented bow to the unions: just weeks before the new $750 million, 1,000-worker Boeing assembly line in South Carolina was set to open, the NLRB filed an action to prevent the opening and tried to force Boeing to shift the production back to its main facility in Washington. The NLRB's drastic action also set up a showdown between the board and the country's twenty-three right-to-work states.*

As some background, right-to-work states guarantee that workers can't be compelled to join unions as a condition of employment at companies that are unionized. There are several reasons workers don't join unions. Two of the biggest are that they don't see the value in the dues or they don't agree with the political activities unions conduct with their dues money or the politicians they support with their endorsements.

The saga with Boeing began when, because of the growing demand for its planes, the company decided to expand its operations and

---

*The twenty-three right-to-work states are Alabama, Arizona, Arkansas, Florida, Georgia, Idaho, Indiana, Iowa, Kansas, Louisiana, Mississippi, Nebraska, Nevada, North Carolina, North Dakota, Oklahoma, South Carolina, South Dakota, Tennessee, Texas, Utah, Virginia, and Wyoming. In December 2012, Michigan became the twenty-fourth right-to-work state.

construct a second assembly plant. The company originally considered constructing the second facility in Washington State. Even though Boeing wasn't required to consult with its union, it tried to work out a deal to build the line there. The deal was, in exchange for all the new union jobs the expansion would create, the machinists would agree to slower growth in their wages and benefits and also a ten-year no-strike clause.

When the machinists union refused the deal in 2009, Boeing decided to build in Charleston, South Carolina. The company cited several reasons for building there, including lower labor costs, financial incentives from the state, and more stability in the production process because its entire workforce wouldn't belong to the union, which meant the chance of strikes and work stoppages would be limited.

Because of that decision, the union charged the company with unfair labor practices. A year later in April 2011, the NLRB filed an action to prevent the opening of the new assembly line.

The NLRB—the federal agency that investigates unfair labor practices—claimed that the new facility would cut back Boeing's unionized workforce in Washington. It also alleged that the decision to build elsewhere was retaliation against the Washington workers for repeatedly striking in the past (four times in a previous ten-year period).

Under federal law, companies aren't allowed to retaliate against union workers for exercising their "right" to strike under the National Labor Relations Act. In this case, the NLRB said the retaliation caused financial harm to union members by taking away jobs they would have had if the plant had been built in Washington. But the fact was that the new South Carolina plant didn't take away any *existing* Washington jobs. In fact, 2,000 new jobs were *created* in Washington after the South Carolina expansion was announced in 2009.

Moreover, the decision to open a plant elsewhere wasn't retaliation for past strikes; rather, it was merely a good business decision to protect the company and ensure that the production of its 787 Dreamliner plane wouldn't fall behind schedule because of any future strikes at the Washington plant (especially when the union wouldn't agree to a ten-year no-strike clause).

But those facts weren't good enough for the Obama administration's labor board. With new Obama appointees, the board was very antibusiness and decidedly pro-union. And the board and its union friends certainly weren't happy with right-to-work states either, because *where union membership is voluntary, unions are simply not as strong.* Many workers—when given the freedom to choose—choose not to join unions. So the NLRB pressed ahead with its case and its intimidation of Boeing.

William Kilberg was Boeing's lead counsel in the case and wrote in the *Wall Street Journal* how the labor board under the Obama administration had been like no previous board in its intimidation and its willingness to flout the law:

> [T]he NLRB case against Boeing is best understood as one in a series of recent administration steps to strengthen unions and weaken companies. . . . The NLRB has experienced ideological swings throughout its existence depending on the party in the White House. But the degree of change and the willingness to ignore statutory language and judicial precedents is unique to the [Obama] administration. An "ends justify the means" attitude toward the law has taken hold at the National Labor Relations Board.

Even the *New York Times* reported the shift in philosophy that came with the change in the board's makeup:

> In what may be the strongest signal yet of the new pro-labor orientation of the National Labor Relations Board

under President Obama, the agency filed a complaint
Wednesday seeking to force Boeing to bring an airplane
production line back to its unionized facilities in Washington State instead of moving the work to a nonunion
plant in South Carolina.

The NLRB's attempt to dictate where Boeing could build its
planes was simply unprecedented and blatant pandering to unions.
But the NLRB agenda was clear: The sanction handed down to the
company was meant not only as a warning for just South Carolina
and the company; it was also an assault on the ability of the country's twenty-three right-to-work states to recruit new industry and
new jobs.

It's very important not to understate what the NLRB was really
doing here. It was trying to intimidate every company in America to
keep them from expanding in right-to-work states, with the goal of
driving them all into the states dominated by their union allies.

That's why several state attorneys general like Pam Bondi of Florida, Sam Olens of Georgia, Greg Abbott of Texas, and I joined together to stand with South Carolina attorney general Alan Wilson to
push back and fight the NLRB's tactics.

A total of nine state attorneys general banded together and called
on the National Labor Relations Board to immediately withdraw its
complaint against Boeing. We wrote a legal brief in support of the
company, helping to develop the case on Boeing's behalf. We also
pointed out that the NLRB's pro-union sanction was actually incred-
ibly shortsighted and wouldn't just hurt right-to-work states, but the
states where union membership was compulsory as well. Why would a
company want to locate in a union state knowing the federal government might later attempt to block its ability to expand elsewhere?

As always, there were critics. There were those in the media who
questioned why Virginia was jumping into a South Carolina fight. If

they had taken some time to think about it, they would have understood that if the NLRB were allowed to go unchallenged in South Carolina, its wrath would eventually come to Virginia and the other right-to-work states, where it would threaten our employers and workers, as well.

Virginia is an ardent right-to-work state, and we got in on the front end of this fight to protect our job creators from being intimidated and to protect our workers' right to choose for themselves whether they wanted to join workplace unions.

However, the challenge would not run its course. In December 2011, the machinists union announced a contract with Boeing that guaranteed the company's newest airplane, the 737 MAX, would be built by union members in Washington State. For that concession, the union withdrew its charge of unfair labor practices, and the NLRB dismissed its complaint.

Unfortunately, the fact that Boeing settled this dispute by offering concessions to its union rather than fighting the NLRB in court meant that the issue of how far the labor relations board could go in its efforts to prevent businesses from locating in right-to-work states wasn't resolved. In the future, unionized companies that want to relocate or expand to right-to-work states might have to budget money for legal fees to fight the NLRB and perhaps "protection money" to pay off unions with concessions to get their agreement to the move. In essence, with the NLRB's backing and Boeing's concessions, unions had been given outrageous and unprecedented influence over future business decisions. Would any unionized company ever again be willing to test the waters by moving into a right-to-work state and face a potential NLRB challenge?

The bullying at the NLRB may have already served its purpose. The Boeing dispute may have inflicted significant damage on job creation in right-to-work states that will take a very long time to undo.

The Second EPA Assault—
Regulating Water as a Pollutant

IN JULY 2012, my office initiated another lawsuit against the out-of-control Environmental Protection Agency when the agency ignored the law yet again in a heavy-handed and costly attempt to control water pollution in Virginia.

For decades, the EPA had at its disposal the Clean Water Act, which it used to clean up rivers, lakes, and streams quite adequately. But that tool didn't seem to satisfy the agency any longer. It wanted to try something new, something bold, something *illegal*.

What was the EPA's innovative new way of controlling water pollution? It tried to regulate water *itself*—the very substance the Clean Water Act was created to protect—as a *pollutant*.

Under the Clean Water Act, pollutants include things like sewage, garbage, chemical waste, and agricultural runoff (but not water). They also include substances like sediment, which builds up on the beds of waterways and can end up harming the aquatic life that lives on those beds. Sediment was the problem the EPA was trying to solve in Virginia.

In 2011, after the EPA found that the level of aquatic life on the Accotink Creek bed in Fairfax County, Virginia, had degraded, it attempted to improve the situation by ordering Virginia to control excessive sediment buildup. The EPA determined the problem wasn't that sediment was being washed into the creek by stormwater running over the land and into the waterway, but rather that the sediment already in the creek bed was being scoured and carried further downstream by stormwater flowing into the creek. The EPA said that water flow was the problem—the more water that flowed, the more sediment that flowed with it.

Under the Clean Water Act, the agency could have lawfully established a maximum daily limit for how much pollutant (sediment) could enter the creek, and measures could have been instituted to abate it. But rather than establish a daily limit for the sediment, the EPA instead chose a more extreme approach and elected to regulate the *amount of water* that flowed into the creek, as if water were the pollutant. (Hey, the carbon dioxide we exhale is now considered a pollutant; why not make the water we drink a pollutant, too?)

Unfortunately for the EPA, the Clean Water Act and the agency's own regulations specifically spell out a comprehensive list of the types of pollutants that it can regulate, and water is *definitely not* one of them.

But that didn't stop the agency from running roughshod over the law. It moved forward to require Fairfax County and the state to cut the creek's maximum water flow (not the sediment flow) *in half*! To achieve that kind of massive reduction, homeowners and business owners near the Accotink would be forced to build structures to capture and retain stormwater from their roofs, driveways, and parking lots to prevent excess runoff into the creek. This edict gave the EPA a new power, effectively allowing it to regulate water runoff (not just pollutant runoff) from private property. Just wait until that power is let loose on the entire American landscape!

Complying with the EPA's edict would also require the state, through the Virginia Department of Transportation (VDOT), to buy or condemn significant amounts of private property—homes, farms, and businesses—so it could build its own stormwater-capture facilities.

Just as with the EPA greenhouse gas case, Republicans and Democrats put partisanship aside and joined forces to fight this unprecedented overreach. VDOT, represented by my office, and the Democrat-controlled Fairfax County Board of Supervisors joined together to challenge the EPA's mandate, not only because the agency didn't have the legal authority to regulate the water flow, but also because its "fix" would have cost hundreds of millions of dollars *more* than to just restore the stream's habitat by simply targeting the actual pollutant itself. The estimated cost to taxpayers for cutting the water flow in that single creek was nearly $300 million. This cost would be on top of the more than $200 million that Fairfax County was already intending to spend on the restoration of the Accotink. And Fairfax has more than thirty similar creeks. What if the EPA decided to include others? That was some painful math, especially if you were a Fairfax County taxpayer.

For a federal government that could print its own money, $300 million was a light lift. But for a locality and a state government that worked with balanced budgets, that extra cost would hit the taxpayers hard. On top of all that, the EPA couldn't even provide reasonable assurances that its expensive scheme would correct the underlying problem!

What was even more unbelievable was that the solution looked as if it would likely *harm* the environment it was trying to protect, because its enormous cost would divert tax dollars that could be spent more effectively on initiatives that would restore the streambed, such as building stabilizers to prevent stream bank erosion.

On December 14, 2012, I argued in federal district court in Alexandria, Virginia, on behalf of VDOT alongside Fairfax County.

The EPA's justification in court for its unprecedented action was that if Congress didn't *explicitly prohibit* it from regulating water as a pollutant then it had the authority to do so. Logic like this might also lead the EPA to conclude that if Congress didn't explicitly prohibit it from invading Mexico, it had the authority to do that, too.

The EPA also claimed that it could regulate water flow because it was a surrogate measure for regulating sediment. Again, we argued that the Clean Water Act didn't allow for the regulation of "surrogates," only pollutants.

On January 3, 2013, federal judge Liam O'Grady ruled that the EPA had exceeded its authority. In his ruling, he said that federal law simply didn't grant EPA the authority it claimed:

The Court sees no ambiguity in the wording of [the

federal Clean Water Act]. EPA is charged with establishing [limits] for the appropriate pollutants; that does not give them the authority to regulate nonpollutants.

Stormwater runoff is not a pollutant, so EPA is not authorized to regulate it.

To the EPA claim that it could regulate water flow as a surrogate for sediment, Judge O'Grady responded:

EPA may not regulate something over which it has no statutorily granted power . . . as a proxy for something over which it is granted power.

If the sediment levels in Accotink Creek have become dangerously high, what better way to address the problem than by limiting the amount of sediment permitted in the creek?

Precisely!

VDOT and Fairfax County weren't pollution villains with some reckless disregard for the environment. They had both made major investments over the last several decades in environmental improvements, and Fairfax County—where I grew up—had a long history of environmental stewardship, including water quality protection initiatives that far exceeded federal requirements.

So why the heavy-handedness from the EPA? Why the disregard for the law in favor of a "solution" that would cost taxpayers hundreds of millions of dollars more and likely harm the environment instead of improve it? We didn't know. And the EPA didn't care.

What we *did* know was that if the EPA had prevailed, such restrictions would have likely spread across Virginia and the nation, resulting in huge costs and seizures of private property in any community with a creek, river, or lake that the EPA decided it wanted to "protect" with its destructive edicts.

CHAPTER 11

THE FCC: A NEW LOW FOR THE FEDERAL GOVERNMENT'S LAWBREAKING

Guard with jealous attention the public liberty.
Suspect every one who approaches that jewel.

—PATRICK HENRY, at the Virginia Convention
to ratify the federal constitution, 1788

ONE OF THE most egregious and alarming overreaches by the federal government came in 2010 when the Federal Communications Commission directly defied Congress and a federal court order declaring that the FCC didn't have the authority to regulate the Internet, yet it issued Internet regulations anyway.

President Obama had made a campaign promise of a regulated Internet: "I'm a big believer in net neutrality. I campaigned on this. I continue to be a strong supporter of it."

One thing you could be sure of, when you heard the administration say something was going to be "neutral," you knew that it was very likely *not* going to be even close to neutral. Don't fall for the words they use. Remember, their dictionary doesn't read like *Webster's*.

So, how far was the Obama administration willing to go to keep his "net neutrality" promise? I'm not sure that, until this FCC action, we had ever seen a federal court so clearly push an agency back in its place, only to have the agency defy the court and proceed with its unlawful power grab regardless.

If the FCC's blatant disregard for the law were allowed to go un-challenged, would other political appointees and unelected bureau-crats in the Obama administration then feel they could ignore the law, congressional limits to their power, and even binding court decisions? Refusing to honor the ruling of a federal court was one of the most serious threats to our divided form of government and its separation of powers doctrine, and therefore, to our liberty. If the highest officials in the land didn't respect the law, then how could the American people be assured those officials would respect their rights, which were safe-guarded by the very rule of law they chose to ignore?

Regulating the Internet

THE FEDERAL COMMUNICATIONS Commission under its chairman, Obama appointee Julius Genachowski, decided in 2010 it would regulate Internet traffic by imposing open-Internet, or "net neutral-ity," regulations on Internet service providers.

Net neutrality is the concept that web surfers should be able to freely visit web sites, view content, and use online applications, all without interference from their high-speed broadband Internet service providers (ISPs). Interference could include blocking or slowing any of those sites or applications. Basically, net neutrality was how the Inter-net had already been working, for the most part with most ISPs, before government regulation.

Although there weren't indications of widespread ISP "interfer-ence" issues, neutrality proponents had pushed the government to create the rules to enforce net neutrality on broadband Internet ser-vice providers. Proponents included not only individuals and govern-ment officials, but major software and e-commerce companies, such as Google, eBay, and Netflix. They petitioned the Federal Commu-nications Commission to create rules to ensure that cable and telecommunications companies such as Comcast and Verizon, which owned and operated broadband networks that brought high-speed Internet into homes and businesses, couldn't use their ownership of those networks to prevent customers from accessing lawful web sites and web applications; couldn't increase or decrease Internet connection speeds to discriminate in favor of some web sites while discouraging the use of others; and couldn't prohibit the attachment of nonharmful devices to the Internet in the home or office, such as wireless routers. Every site, every application, every appliance was to be treated the same—neutrally.

Proponents of net neutrality feared that, if given the opportunity, ISPs might ultimately discriminate to block competitors' web sites, charge premiums to popular sites just so surfers could access them, or slow speeds to web sites that were data-intensive to discourage their use. Since the very beginning of the public's use of the Internet, anyone could set up a web site, and virtually anyone surfing the web could access it. Proponents of net neutrality were concerned that ISPs would interfere with web users' ability to connect with and use particular web sites for any of a variety of reasons.

This is how one advocacy group, Free Press, described why it thought net neutrality regulations were necessary:

> The biggest cable and telephone companies would like to charge money for smooth access to Web sites, speed to run applications, and permission to plug in devices. These network giants believe they should be able to charge Web site operators, application providers and device manufacturers for the right to use the network. Those who don't make a deal and pay up will experience discrimination: Their sites won't load as quickly, and their applications and devices won't work as well. Without legal protection, consumers could find that a network operator has

blocked the Web site of a competitor, or slowed it down so much that it's unusable.

So What Was the Problem with Net Neutrality? It Sounded Like a Good Idea

HERITAGE FOUNDATION SENIOR research fellow James Gattuso wrote in 2009 that government-imposed net neutrality would result in

> a slower and more congested Internet, and more frustration for users. Even worse, investment in expanding the Internet will be chilled, as FCC control of network management makes investment less inviting. The amounts at stake aren't trivial, with tens of billions invested each year in Internet expansion.

The ISPs claimed they had a legitimate need for the option to block or slow large data transmissions from certain data-intensive web sites such as streaming movie sites and music download sites. Many ISPs worried that they couldn't adequately regulate "Internet hogs"—those who used a disproportionate share of the Internet pipeline because they used or exchanged large amounts of data. ISPs felt that without the ability to slow down data speeds for web sites and applications that put high loads on their networks, other customers who shared the Internet pipeline would experience slower Internet speeds. Except for a few select circumstances, the new FCC rules didn't allow Internet service providers to manage the flow of data traffic on their own networks as they saw fit.

As an example, think of the network that brings the Internet to your house as being similar to the city water pipe that brings water to your house. Only so much water can flow through the pipe at one time, and if your neighbors are all using large amounts of water at the same time you are, the amount of water coming out of your faucet may be reduced to a trickle. To prevent that from happening and ensuring that you and your neighbors have at least a minimum flow from your faucets, the water company might install a system that limits the amount of water that any one house can take out of the pipeline at any one time. Then someone who decides to turn on all the faucets in his house at once can't do a lot to disrupt the water flow at your house. In the same way, ISPs may sometimes choose to block or slow applications that use a lot of data and slow down their networks for other users.

Another issue that net neutrality advocates failed to take into account was that Internet service providers owned the pipelines that got people on the Internet, which made this a private property rights issue, too.

A government agency—the FCC—without the authority to do so, was attempting to dictate to broadband providers how they had to use their own private property—the pipelines and technology that brought us the Internet.

The ISPs invested billions of dollars a year to build their network pipelines out and develop newer, faster technologies. Although we all wanted an open Internet where we could freely visit any site we wanted, we needed to remember that we were using someone else's property to get there. The government couldn't just seize that property through regulation to use it how it saw fit . . . but that didn't stop the FCC from trying!

We rightly balk when the government seizes a home and turns it over to a private developer to build a mall because that is offensive to our notion of property rights. This situation is very much the same. Although some people want a mall or an open Internet and don't care how they get them, in a free society such as ours, this "ends justify the means" philosophy is antithetical to liberty.

Competition, Not Regulation, Was the Key
to Protecting an Open Internet

B UT THE BIGGEST issue with net neutrality was that competition, not regulation, was the key to protecting the idea of an open Internet.

There was no systemic market failure that had occurred on the Internet that demanded new government oversight. In fact, the rapid innovation and financial investment in broadband came about precisely because under both Republican and Democrat presidents and congresses, the government was careful to stay out of the way while a competitive free market experimented with new ideas. The Internet has been one of the freest of the free markets.

Companies worked both collaboratively and competitively to create new hardware and applications to meet consumer demand for ever-evolving technology—faster, smaller, more powerful, and with more features. These innovations required lots of investment, and because the potential financial returns were so incredible, the investment was often worth the risk.

To use government mandates to change what had worked so well for so long risked severely impairing the greatest economic and innovation engine history has ever seen. One of the best ways to dis-incentivize new investment was to create a new regulatory regime to handcuff it.

Furthermore, free-market competition among Internet service providers for customers regulated ISPs better than the government ever could: if ISPs decided to slow access, charge more for different levels of usage, or prohibit access to certain high-bandwidth-usage sites, customers could switch to other providers. Competition among providers and consumers' ability to choose the providers that best met their needs (that is, liberty in practice)—not the government's ability to regulate the Internet—would force ISPs to remain consumer-friendly and would protect consumers from abuses by network operators.

If the FCC ends up prevailing and is allowed to move forward with net neutrality regulations, Internet innovation will undoubtedly drop dramatically as the government starts to interfere with how the pipeline should work, investors move to other opportunities, and ISPs are less profitable and therefore have less money with which to innovate. That could mean ISPs would leave the industry, which would leave fewer providers, fewer choices for consumers, and inevitably higher prices for slower Internet access. In other words, government intervention—as it usually does—is most likely to follow the law of unintended consequences and produce the exact opposite of the intended effect.

The Biggest Problem with Net Neutrality: The FCC Was Breaking the Law

THIS LEGAL SHOWDOWN with the FCC began in 2008, when the agency said that Internet service provider Comcast Corporation broke the law when it lowered the download speeds for certain customers accessing large video files on the Internet. Comcast said its actions were necessary because those customers were dragging down Internet speeds for other customers sharing the pipeline. The FCC claimed it had the authority to regulate Comcast because Congress had long ago given it the authority to regulate telephone companies, and it assumed that by extension, somehow it also had the authority to regulate broadband Internet service providers, too.

The FCC was reaching, and in April 2010, the U.S. Court of Appeals for the District of Columbia Circuit ruled that Congress never gave it the authority to regulate broadband Internet providers and that the agency couldn't block ISPs from taking active steps to manage their networks by regulating the bandwidth of their high-volume users. The FCC did not appeal that ruling.

Not only did Congress never grant the FCC the power to regulate the Internet, Congress had also repeatedly rejected passing net neutrality legislation. Thus the FCC tried to assume for itself a power that our elected representatives in Congress wouldn't even take for themselves.

Despite the DC circuit court ruling, in December 2010—after most members of Congress had left town—three of the five FCC commissioners said they were going to regulate the Internet anyway and approved new net neutrality regulations for cable television and telephone companies that provided high-speed Internet access. Once again, the Obama administration had circumvented Congress—and this time, defied the courts—to push its unpopular policy agenda on the American people.

In early 2011, I began to discuss with several of my attorney general colleagues how to stop the FCC's unprecedented and lawless takeover of the Internet. However, since the state governments weren't directly harmed by the net neutrality regulations, we weren't able to bring suit.

In 2012, telecommunications company Verizon filed suit against the FCC in the case of *Verizon v. FCC*. That's when attorneys general Sam Olens of Georgia, Bill Schuette of Michigan, Scott Pruitt of Oklahoma, Alan Wilson of South Carolina, Darrell McGraw of West Virginia, and I joined together to file our friend-of-the-court brief. A friend-of-the-court (or amicus) brief is one in which the brief writer is not one of the parties involved in the suit but is helping the court by presenting a legal analysis about why one side in the dispute should prevail over the other.

Although the issues of property rights, free-market competition, and maintaining network speeds were important, I only mentioned them earlier for some background. Whether one agreed with the concept of net neutrality didn't matter to the states in this case. Our argument wasn't over whether the open Internet was good public policy. From a legal perspective, we were fighting the FCC over one legal issue: it had assumed a power Congress never gave it, and then when it was told to stop exercising that power by a federal court, it ignored the court and proceeded anyway.

In our brief, we argued that by providing broadband Internet services, telecommunication companies weren't providing the "telecommunication services" (telephone service) that were subject to mandatory FCC regulation under the law. Instead, when the companies were providing broadband Internet services, they fell within the classification of "information service" providers, which clearly weren't subject to FCC regulation. The FCC couldn't just declare out of thin air that it had regulatory powers it was never granted.

If the FCC wanted to legally and constitutionally contest whether it had the authority to regulate the Internet, it should have appealed the court ruling of April 2010. Instead, the FCC just disregarded it.

Even if you are a supporter of net neutrality, no one should be a supporter of a government that breaks the law in order to force regulations on the American people, no matter how well intentioned. Defying a court order to issue those regulations was a new high-water mark for government overreach and a serious threat to liberty. I will say it again: If the federal government has such disrespect for the rule of law, how can the people be assured their government will ultimately have any respect for their rights, which are protected under the law?

As of this writing, the Verizon case is still pending before the circuit court.

CHAPTER 12

SHOULDER-TO-SHOULDER ON
THE LAST LINE OF DEFENSE

||||||||||||||||||||||||||||||||||||||||||||||||||||||||||||||||||||||||||||||||||||||||||||||||||||||||||

The truth is, all might be free if they valued
freedom, and defended it as they ought.

—SAMUEL ADAMS, 1771

And the Federalism Battles Continued . . .

ON MARCH 5, 2012, nine attorneys general* from across the country who had been working together to battle the illegal overreaches of the federal government met in Washington, DC, to discuss future strategy. While we were together, I organized a news conference so we could report to the American people the pattern that had emerged of a near total disregard for the laws of the nation by a president who had sworn to uphold those very laws. The people needed to understand the government's unprecedented lawbreaking and what was at stake if President Obama were reelected. If the "bolder," more controversial initiatives were usually saved for a president's second term when he didn't have to worry about reelection, we were all concerned about what lay ahead.

While each of the nine attorneys general had his or her own *policy*

---

*Greg Abbott from Texas, Pam Bondi from Florida, Tom Horne from Arizona, Alan Wilson from South Carolina, Sam Olens from Georgia, Bill Schuette from Michigan, Scott Pruitt from Oklahoma, Marty Jackley from South Dakota, and me.

and *political* disagreements with President Obama, those disagreements weren't what brought us together that day. The Obama administration had made plenty of decisions that we believed were flawed policy, but that didn't make them illegal. As attorneys general, we were there to talk about the administration's disrespect for the law, and the law alone.

While the health care case was what had received the most attention before the news conference, it was merely representative of a much larger pattern. Citing offenses by the EPA, the FCC, the National Labor Relations Board, the White House, and others, the attorneys general clearly laid out the Obama administration's pattern of aggressively using administrative agencies to implement policy objectives that couldn't gain congressional approval and were outside the law.

President Obama and his appointees had continually ignored federal laws, binding rulings of federal courts, and the limits on their power mandated by the Constitution. His executive agencies were waging an across-the-board regulatory assault on the states and their citizens. It was all to make government work in ways they couldn't achieve through the normal democratic process.

The *Wall Street Journal* reinforced this very point when it editorialized about a federal court's striking down "another misguided EPA rule"—the Cross-State Air Pollution Rule that Texas attorney general Greg Abbott and other states had been fighting:

> House Republicans are making the case that Obama regulators have been punishing U.S. business in violation of the law and beyond what Congress intended. Tuesday's ruling proves their point and underscores how much more damaging the EPA could be without reelection restraint in a second Obama term.
>
> The court's decision states it plainly: "Absent a claim of constitutional authority (and there is none here), executive agencies may exercise only the authority conferred

by statute, and agencies may not transgress statutory limits on that authority."

The message is that regulators must follow the laws
of the United States. Why do federal judges constantly
have to remind EPA Administrator Lisa Jackson of this
basic principle?

At the time of the news conference, just those nine attorneys
general alone had already cataloged twenty-one violations of the law
that the administration had committed and which we were fighting in
court. But the federal abuses of power went beyond even that, because
at that time, more than thirty states were in the process of suing the
federal government for overstepping its authority. In addition to the
violations that I've already covered in this book, such as the FCC,
the Office of Surface Mining, and the health care suit, following are a
few more instances—it's not even an all-inclusive list—to demonstrate
the breadth of the lawbreaking:

- *The Environmental Protection Agency:* Florida already had
  some of the most aggressive water quality protection programs in the country, yet the EPA decided to preempt them
  and impose its own unprecedented and unscientific standards, which would have cost the Sunshine State billions in
  compliance, significant spikes in utility bills, and the loss of
  thousands of jobs. A federal judge found that the EPA rule
  wasn't even based on sound science and that the agency
  failed to prove that the rule would prevent harm to the environment, which in and of itself was a direct violation of law.
- *The Department of Justice:* Under the Voting Rights Act of
  1965, the U.S. attorney general and his DOJ are responsible
  for reviewing all changes to voter laws of certain states.
  The DOJ rejected Arizona's and South Carolina's voter

identification laws, which were enacted to curb voter fraud and were similar to those *already approved* by the U.S. Supreme Court. The laws required voters to show photo identification or some other proof that they were simply who they claimed to be for purposes of voting or, absent that, to simply complete an affidavit to vote.

- *The National Labor Relations Board:* The NLRB threatened to sue South Carolina when voters approved a state constitutional amendment guaranteeing a secret ballot for employees voting whether to unionize their workplaces. Unions don't like secret ballots, as they prefer to know how workers are going to vote. Secret ballots guarantee that employees can vote their consciences instead of voting out of fear of retribution from union bosses. When three other states with similar state constitutional amendments joined South Carolina in mounting a defense, the NLRB backed down from all the states except Arizona, where it moved forward with its suit.

- *The Environmental Protection Agency again:* The EPA tried to regulate air pollution in Texas under its new Cross-State Air Pollution Rule, after it claimed that a significant amount of Texas's air pollution from older coal power plants was crossing over into other states. EPA roped the state into the regulations at the last minute and without giving Texas the required time under the law to respond to the proposed rule. In addition, the application of the cross-state rule to Texas was based on a dubious claim that air pollution from Texas had affected *one* single air-quality monitor in Illinois—more than 500 miles and three states away. Additionally, Congress had set up a cooperative federalism-based system of air pollution control in which the federal government set air quality standards for pollutants and the states had the primary responsibility for determining how to meet those standards within their borders. The EPA totally disregarded that cooperative arrangement when unilaterally mandating the rules on twenty-eight states.

- *The Department of Justice again:* The U.S. attorney general and his DOJ sued both Arizona and South Carolina to prevent the states from enforcing federal immigration laws that the federal government refused to enforce itself. In fact, Congress passed immigration laws with the clear intent that states would assist the government with enforcement, but the Obama administration attacked states that were trying to help restore the rule of law in the immigration arena. In its attacks, the federal government tried to publicly raise the specter that these new state laws would lead to racial profiling, but DOJ lawyers actually admitted in court that they didn't have any real claim of such profiling. The bottom line is that states welcome *legal* immigrants, and to not control illegal immigration and turn a blind eye to lawlessness is unfair to those immigrants who come to this country playing by the rules.

- *The White House:* President Obama ignored the Constitution when he *claimed* the U.S. Senate was in recess when it wasn't (it was still in session according to the Constitution, though on a three-day break) so that he could make three controversial appointments to the National Labor Relations Board and one appointment to the Consumer Financial Protection Bureau and avoid the constitutionally prescribed Senate confirmation process for his appointees—presumably because he didn't think they'd get approved.

At that news conference, the nine state attorneys general committed to continue working in a united front. We would serve as a de facto task force, assisting one another to defend state laws and identifying "best practices" and legal arguments to fight back against the administration's disregard for the law.

My colleagues and I were there that day because too many Washington politicians—regardless of party—had failed to adhere to the Constitution and the rule of law, starting with the president himself.

However, the blame didn't fall solely on the Obama administration. If Congress had had the will, it could have stopped some of the illegal overreaches by voting to defund the offending agencies. But because there wasn't that will, it fell to state attorneys general to push back against the government in court.

As the *Washington Examiner* said in an editorial after the news conference:

> Elections are just one way the Constitution empowers Americans to fight back against a centralizing regime in the nation's capital. State attorneys general have every right—indeed, it is their obligation—to respond forcefully when the federal government breaks the law.

CHAPTER 13

THE LIBERTY PIE

||||||||||||||||||||||||||||||||||||||||||||||||||||||||||||||||||||||||||||||||||||||||||||||||||||||||||||||||||||||||||||

*I believe there are more instances of the abridgment of the
freedom of the people by gradual and silent encroachments of
those in power, than by violent and sudden usurpations.*

—JAMES MADISON at the Virginia Convention
to ratify the federal constitution, 1788

UNDER PRESIDENT BARACK OBAMA, the federal government had
moved beyond just growing bigger, more powerful, and more expensive. Instead, it had gotten to a point where those in government
were repeatedly disregarding the law to force unprecedented liberty-
and economy-destroying policies on the American people.

This lawlessness may have been an inevitable evolution for government, because even before President Obama, the country had
long strayed from the founding principles that once kept the government in check. For generations, government had become more and
more distant from the limited power guardian of liberty it once was.
Most citizens had become used to it taking a larger share of their
incomes and creating more intrusive rules for their lives so it could
meet the growing demands to be a universal problem-solver and national nanny. As a result, the sad reality was that, over time, we had
become accustomed to letting our liberties be eroded without a fight.

People who sounded the alarm about the dangers of big government and who wanted to return to the principles that made the United

States the freest and most prosperous nation in the history of the world were often dismissed as "fringe" and "outside the mainstream" by the statists who liked to use big government to achieve their political and societal agendas. Some in the media who shared the statists' agendas ensured that this distorted image of small-government conservatives and libertarians also became cemented in the minds of everyday citizens in an attempt to marginalize those who argued against their ideas. They said we wanted to throw grandmothers off Medicare, push the poor into the streets, pollute the air and the water, and make sure that children didn't get educated.

Those kinds of inane slurs all sound absurd when you first hear them, but when they're repeated over and over about Republicans, libertarians, conservatives, and Tea Party activists by politicians and those in the media whom the public trusts, people start to believe the propaganda.

After President Obama was first elected, the federal government perpetuated those same distortions. The Department of Homeland Security issued a 2009 report that warned about the possibility of violence and domestic terrorism by "right-wing extremists," who we were told could be people concerned about illegal immigration, the growth of federal power, and bans on firearms, and who may "[reject] federal authority in favor of state or local authority." They made it sound as though any citizen concerned about constitutional government or liberty could be considered a right-wing extremist and a potential domestic terrorist.

But average citizens began to realize that small-government advocates had good reason to sound the alarm bells when they started to witness for themselves the Obama administration's repeated disregard for the law and the Constitution so it could force its destructive policy goals on the American people.

Now that more citizens are listening, how can we turn this ship of state around? How can we ensure that government will continue to safeguard our precious liberties rather than issue more onerous regulations and taxes to usurp them? How can we guarantee that government creates an environment for a vibrant and growing economy that lifts the prosperity of *all*, rather than *destroys* the incentives that drive entrepreneurship, wealth creation, and jobs? How can we guarantee that the people will remain the ultimate sovereigns—the ones who ultimately possess the supreme political power—and that the government will work for them, not the other way around?

First, we must have determination and patience. We didn't get into this situation overnight, so it will take time to get out of it. Second, we need to remember two basic concepts that serve as reminders of what government's relationship with its people is *supposed* to be, of the first principles that made this nation great, and of the formula to achieve greater personal liberty and a growing economy. These two concepts are the economic pie and the liberty pie.

The Economic Pie

P RESIDENT RONALD REAGAN made famous what he called the "economic pie." The economic pie represented the entire American economy that was shared by citizens, businesses, and government. The more robust the economy, the bigger the pie grew. The tighter the economy, the smaller the pie was, with less available to everyone. While many felt that the only thing you could do was cut the slices small enough to spread the pie around to all people, Ronald Reagan understood that the economy had nearly unlimited potential for growth, and that you could make the pie bigger if government didn't stand in the way of the free market. And history proved him right.

Decades before becoming president, Mr. Reagan had railed against the federal government's growing habit of cutting an increasing number of slices from the nation's economic pie for itself—taking from the people much more money than it needed just to sustain its basic functions. Every new federal program meant a new slice taken from the economy. The bigger slices were failing federal programs that "needed" more and more money to keep functioning, regardless of their inefficiency or ineffectiveness.

Mr. Reagan criticized government for taxing hardworking and productive Americans to pay for every slice of pie that the government took and then used in ever more inefficient ways. All of this slicing left less and less of the economic pie for ordinary, taxpaying Americans who were earning their piece of the pie the old-fashioned way—with hard work.

President Reagan also talked about the sheer foolishness of the federal government's reliance on propping up the economy by redistributing wealth from the productive to the unproductive. That didn't grow the economy. All that accomplished was to shift around a limited amount of money, rather than create new wealth. In fact, it even had the unintended consequence of *shrinking* the economy, as it reduced a productive person's incentive to create new wealth because so much of it would be taken away from him in the form of higher taxes.

Instead of following that failed model, President Reagan believed that we grew the economy—and increased the size of the pie—by helping the unproductive become productive. In other words, don't give them a fish, but teach them how to fish. He said:

> The weakness in this country for too many years has been our insistence on carving an ever-increasing number of slices from a shrinking economic pie. Our policies have concentrated on rationing scarcity rather than creating plenty. As a result, our economy has stagnated. But those days are ending. We must lift where we stand, struggle for tomorrow, and earn anew the reputation this country once had as the land of golden opportunity.

He also said:

> Instead of fighting over who gets the last piece of a
> shrinking economic pie, let's help America produce a
> bigger pie so that everyone will have a chance to be bet-
> ter off.

President Reagan explained that government played an enormous role in helping our nation's economy to grow or in condemning it to shrink by its choice of which fiscal policies to implement. For our fortieth president, getting government out of the way of people and businesses was the best way the government could help the economy grow.

Ladies and gentlemen, the greatness of America happened because—compared with the rest of the world—Americans were mostly free from government control, and that type of freedom created an environment that allowed us to reach more of our potential than we could anywhere else in the world.

But what does it mean to "get government out of the way"? It means repealing regulations in which the costs to the American people and to the American economy outweigh the benefits, especially when the benefits are unproven at best, or actually burdens at worst. It means simplifying the tax code so that individuals and companies aren't wasting billions of hours and billions of dollars each year merely to file taxes and comply with tax laws, when that time and money could be more productively spent growing American prosperity.

Astonishingly, according to the National Taxpayers Union, in 2012, complying with our complex tax code cost Americans 6.38 billion hours of work per year—the equivalent of more than *three million* employees working 40-hour workweeks year-round! That's a lot of wasted productivity that could have been spent developing and producing new products and services for the American economy.

Finally, getting government out of the way means reducing

government spending so we can reduce the crushing burden of taxes and leave more money in the hands of the American people—those who know better how to spend it than politicians and bureaucrats.

President Reagan's economic pie argument focused primarily on taxes and secondarily on regulations. He told us that government shrank the economic pie when it increased taxes or regulations, which dragged down the economy. And a smaller economic pie meant less prosperity for everyone.

He pointed out, however, that when government reduced taxes and regulations, it cleared impediments to America's potential, allowing freedom and opportunity to blossom, and with them, a growing economic pie. A bigger pie meant more prosperity for *everyone:* more wealth, more consumer spending, and more jobs and higher wages to meet increased consumer demand.

Although this way of governing has already been proven to work in our economy and even to help the poorest in society, it's still a challenge for some because not everyone will get the same size slice of pie, nor will everyone's slice increase by the same amount. But while some would have much more than others, those who had the least would still have more than they ever had before.

As Winston Churchill wisely noted:

> The inherent vice of capitalism is the unequal sharing of the blessings. The inherent blessing of socialism is the equal sharing of misery.

The decade before Ronald Reagan's presidency demonstrated Churchill's "equal sharing of misery" scenario very clearly: by the time President Reagan took office, America was in the middle of an energy crisis, complete with oil and gasoline shortages; consumer inflation was at 13 percent; the prime lending rate was 20 percent (that was the interest rate for the most creditworthy; for those with lower credit, the rate was much higher); and the top marginal income tax rate was 70 percent. President Jimmy Carter had blamed the American people, telling them they were experiencing "a crisis of confidence. It is a crisis that strikes at the very heart and soul and spirit of our national will."

We've seen the experiments in socialism and in the less onerous democratic socialism around the world, where ensuring that everyone gets the same has only led to stagnant or collapsing economies and poverty and misery. Just look at the failing economies of Greece and Spain and other European countries in which they experienced soaring unemployment, out-of-control inflation, and public unrest that led to riots in the streets. The lessons from those experiments are clear: Americans are better off contending with the envy of plenty than with the desperation of scarcity.

Another of Ronald Reagan's lessons is also clear: when government lowers taxes, stops trying to redistribute wealth among the citizenry, and leaves more money in the hands of the people rather than in government coffers, charitable giving increases and grows the social safety net for the truly needy among us.

Mr. Reagan recognized capitalism's blessings and socialism's misery, which explains part of why he was so passionate about growing America's economic pie—so that virtually everyone could enjoy *more* prosperity. And because he succeeded, America experienced one of the deepest and longest economic expansions in our history.

The Liberty Pie

ECONOMIC WELL-BEING IS important, but even before the economy comes liberty. So, what about the *liberty pie?*

The liberty pie is an analogy I created to illustrate the relationship between the individual and government. Like the economic pie, it, too, looks at taxes, regulations, and spending, but it looks at how those factors affect our liberty rather than our economy. Unlike the economic pie, however, the liberty pie never changes size. It never grows or shrinks, and it has only two slices: government power and citizens' liberty. What changes are the sizes of the slices.

Every single thing government does to increase its own power increases the size of *its slice* of the liberty pie. Since there are only two slices, every time the government's slice of the liberty pie grows, the citizens' slice is *reduced*.

This makes sense if we remember that our government derives its power from the people. We created our government, and we delegated to it some of our authority to do the things we charged it to do. Each time we ask the government to do more things, we turn over more power to it, and, naturally, our liberty is reduced. The problem is that today, rather than the citizens' willingly *giving* power to the government, the government has grown powerful enough to *take* power from us. The battles I have written about in this book—from health care to the EPA to the FCC—clearly illustrate that.

There are three ways government grows its own power and thus shrinks our liberty: more regulations, more taxation, and more spending.

It's easy to understand how more government regulation of our lives and businesses reduces our freedom: it takes away our choices or compels us to do things. Regulations and laws are government directives that tell people and businesses what to do or not do.

It's equally simple to see how taking more of our money through higher taxes reduces our freedom: we can't keep all the money we earn, so we can't spend it or give it away as we choose.

Finally, we can see that increased government spending reduces our liberty, not just by forcing the government to increase taxes now or on future generations to pay for that spending, but also by competing with and crowding out private businesses and other organizations (e.g., churches) when it does things the private sector can and should do instead.

Of course, some regulation, some government spending, and some taxation are necessary to have an operational government in a free society. But the point is that each of these things, even in the smallest doses, comes at the expense of liberty, so whenever government thinks about increasing any of them, we need to remember that it will come at an even greater cost to our liberty—and we should always weigh that cost carefully before proceeding.

Regulations

REGULATIONS IN THIS context include laws and are commands by government that you must obey or face fines or criminal prosecution. For individuals, examples of laws and regulations include the compulsion to buy private health insurance or pay a tax; the prohibition against building on private property if it has a semipermanent puddle that allows it to be categorized as a wetland; the prohibition on carrying a gun to protect oneself and one's family; or the requirement to use only government-approved building materials when remodeling your home. Every action that government forbids you from taking, every action that government compels you to undertake, reduces your liberty. The more government regulates, the less free people are.

Laws and regulations also burden businesses. Laws tell businesses whether they should give preferences to more expensive union labor when contracting out work; how much banks can charge to retailers for credit card fees; how Internet service providers can and can't use their own network equipment; and how much businesses must pay their workers (establishing *both* upper and lower limits).

The costs to businesses to comply with regulations don't just hurt business owners, they also harm average citizens by raising the prices of food, clothing, and shelter (as regulatory costs are inevitably passed on to consumers); by reducing jobs (as businesses have less money left over to hire more people); and by reducing businesses' ability to pursue new growth opportunities (which could grow the economy and create more jobs).

Let's take a very simple example of a regulation many people find unnecessary. State governments often impose training and licensing requirements on people who want to become barbers.

Come on, people cut hair in their homes all the time without being licensed, and they seem pretty competent! And I don't know about you, but my own firsthand experience proves that training and government licensing requirements do not automatically lead to good haircuts. I'm also not going to die from a bad haircut, so why is it so critical to have a licensing process?

Some will ask, "Without licensing, how are we supposed to pick a barber?" Well first, I know I don't keep going back to a barber who messed up my last haircut. If barbers don't do good work, they lose business. Word spreads. Soon, the bad barbers go out of business.

So why license barbers if free choices in the free market will weed out the lousy barbers? The weed-out process happens without reducing anyone's freedom (the barber's freedom to go into business, and the consumers' freedom to have their hair cut by whomever they want).

In addition, many professional associations offer voluntary accreditation that demonstrates that the person has certain skills and has achieved certain standards of workmanship. If consumers want to know that someone is qualified for the job, they can look specifically for those who have been accredited. This provides a free-market alternative to licensing and replaces expensive government bureaucracies that have to use the force of regulation to mandate licensing requirements.

Additionally, any time you impose hurdles on people's activities, like becoming a barber, you prevent a certain proportion of folks from achieving—or even pursuing—that career. Why? Because some people can't afford the classes or licensing fees, or they can't spare the time for the classes (even though they may have apprenticed at the feet of masters), or they can't spare the time to wade through the additional government paperwork requirements associated with the licensing.

Why would we create more barriers to prevent folks from building careers and incomes? Creating more barriers means a potentially thriving business may never come into being—a business that might have created new jobs, given the unemployed new opportunities, and grown the economy of a small neighborhood.

But these liberty-reducing regulations don't just hurt the person who doesn't become a barber or the employees he never got to hire; they also hurt consumers by eliminating a number of good barbers from the marketplace. These regulatory burdens limit the number of competitors in the marketplace, which means a smaller supply of barbers and therefore overall higher prices and lower-quality haircuts. More barbers competing for customers means that prices go down and the quality of the haircuts goes up as barbers try to draw customers through their doors.

For consumers, the liberty part of this example is that more barbers equals more choices. The economic part is that more barbers equals higher-quality service and lower prices. Liberty and economy are inseparable. You never have an effect on one without an effect on the other.

If this sounds like too minor of an example to be concerned about, consider how many hundreds of thousands of regulations exist in this country—from licensing barbers, to licensing family farmers to sell their products on the roadside, to securing government permission to add a new piece of medical equipment to your local hospital—and all the opportunities that are made more difficult to pursue (in other words, the reduction of liberty) because of those regulations.

The American Action Forum is a policy institute that catalogs the increasing burden of regulations on Americans and American businesses. The AAF calculated that the new federal regulations created *in just 2011 alone* imposed $232 billion in *new* annual costs to comply with them and 133 million *more* hours annually to fill out paperwork. Remember, those are not cumulative totals for the last ten or twenty years; those are *new* burdens in one year alone!

That's $232 billion of lost money and opportunities . . . and a lot of lost liberty pie and lost economic pie.

That's also 133 million hours spent doing paperwork that people and businesses didn't voluntarily choose to do. More lost liberty pie.

With all this time and money spent complying with government regulations, when is there time and money left for businesses to actually *do business?*

Big-government proponents would love you to believe that corporations need all this regulation because they are made up of greedy, evil people (some are greedy and/or evil; most aren't) who just want to pollute the environment, defraud consumers, and make money off the backs of the vulnerable men and women who work for them. They try to make you forget that these "greedy" corporations contribute to the economy through their taxes; through the goods and services they buy from vendors; by providing goods and services that people want or need; and by creating jobs for working men and women to go to each day. Those jobs allow those working men and women to provide their families with homes, food, clothing, cars, and college funds.

Big-government proponents also don't understand that, as economist Milton Friedman states below, free markets are an excellent force to keep businesses in line. If a company is polluting the ground and its waste is seeping into a neighbor's property, the neighbor can sue for damages. If the company is using cheap materials in production or is treating its employees badly, employees can leave, and consumers can force it to change its practices by ceasing to do business with it, encouraging others to do the same, and by patronizing its competition.

People and markets aren't perfect. There *is* a role for government to keep companies and people from defrauding one another. But we should be wary of too much government control, as we have today. Milton Friedman explained why we should have less faith in government control and more faith in the free market in his 1962 book *Capitalism and Freedom:*

> So long as effective freedom of exchange is maintained, the central feature of the market organization of economic activity is that it prevents one person from interfering with another in respect of most of his activities. The consumer is protected from coercion by the seller because of the presence of other sellers with whom he can deal. The seller is protected from coercion by the consumer because of other consumers to whom he can sell. The employee is protected from coercion by the employer because of other employers for whom he can work, and so on. And the market does this impersonally and without centralized authority.
>
> Indeed, a major source of objection to a free economy is precisely that it does this task so well. It gives people what they want instead of what a particular group thinks they ought to want. Underlying most arguments against the free market is a lack of belief in freedom itself.

Whether it's by the gradual layering on of regulations that make it too expensive to continue a business (or at least to continue it in this country . . .), or by the imposition of barriers that are too high for some to climb over to start a business, or by denying consumers buying choices, regulations can often be more destructive than protective, and they always reduce liberty. So any time a regulation is proposed, a strict and realistic cost-benefit analysis should be performed to judge whether the liberty we're losing is worth "the good" expected as a result of our sacrifice.

Spending

I NCREASING GOVERNMENT SPENDING might be the least obvious way government reduces your slice of the liberty pie. But government spending reduces liberty in three key ways:

1. Unlike business spending and personal spending—both of which can increase the economic growth of the nation (and thereby create more jobs, greater incomes, and greater prosperity)—government spending may increase growth somewhat, but *never* to the degree of the private sector, if for no other reason than because of the high degree of inefficiency in how government spends money.
2. Increased spending crowds out private-sector activity, either directly, by doing what the private sector would otherwise do, or indirectly, by borrowing the money that would otherwise be available to the private sector.
3. Increased government spending requires either higher current taxes or higher future taxes to pay for that spending. (I'll talk about this later under the taxation section.)

A simple example of how private-sector spending increases economic growth more than government spending does would be a business that smartly spends $100 and expects to earn that amount back plus a return on its investment, so it turns $100 into, let's say, $115. That's economic growth.

In contrast, despite how many times you may hear politicians talk about "investments" in government programs, government spends very little on what you could call "investments" that result in economic growth. For example, in 2011, the biggest programs in the federal government were Social Security (20 percent of the budget), national defense (20 percent), and Medicare (13.5 percent). There is no monetary return on these investments in any traditional business sense (that is, one invests money with a goal of getting a return in the form of interest, income, or appreciation in value), although there are obviously other reasons America spends money on these programs.

I'm not questioning here the existence of these programs nor the wisdom of how much money is spent on them. What I'm trying to illustrate is that most dollars that government spends do not create economic growth but instead take money out of the hands of the people who *do* create economic growth. For that reason, if we want to grow our economy, if we want to grow job opportunities, if we want to grow our national prosperity and raise up *all* people, we have to be cautious about how much we take from the private sector—the economic growth sector—and give to the government sector to spend.

Another problem with government spending is the mistaken thinking that its taking and spending the people's money will stimulate the economy better than the people's spending it themselves. The economy is made up of hundreds of millions of people exercising their freedom to make hundreds of millions of decisions to undertake hundreds of millions of individual economic transactions each day. That's an enormous number of economic decisions that power the economy, which a central planning government using the most powerful computer in the world could never even come close to replicating. Since *we, the people* are also *we, the market*, we know better than government what we like and don't like, what we want to buy and don't want to buy, and which companies will get our business and which won't. Our individual choices determine which companies will be the winners and the losers in the marketplace and which products will be hits and which will be duds. That's why the individuals who make up the market know how to spend their own money—and therefore, stimulate the economy—better than government does.

One example of this economic truth was when President Obama used billions of taxpayer dollars to "stimulate" green energy companies like Solyndra during the economic downturn. When Solyndra lacked enough private investors and lacked demand for its products, that was the market—i.e., the people—telling us that this was not a company that should stay in business. Despite that clear message, the government was willing to put hundreds of millions of taxpayer dollars into it. The company eventually went bankrupt, and our dollars were wasted because the market knew better how to spend that money than the government.

The second reason increased government spending reduces our liberty is because it crowds out private-sector activity. This crowding out happens in two ways: the government borrows money to spend that would otherwise be available to the private sector, and the government competes with the private sector by offering services or products that the private sector would otherwise offer (running recreation centers and liquor stores, for example).

In the first instance, government spending crowds out business opportunities by borrowing a lot of the money that it spends. The good old Economics 101 supply-and-demand curve applies to money just as it does to corn or gas or anything else that's bought and sold. Put simply, when the government borrows large sums of money, it has increased the demand for money; and when you increase demand for something, you increase its price. The price for money is the interest rate you're charged when you borrow it. So, when the federal government borrows large sums of money, the increased demand causes the interest rates for everyone else to go up. "Everyone else" includes private individuals and private businesses. This increased cost of borrowing stifles private-sector borrowing and means that consumers have less to spend and businesses (which rely heavily on borrowing) have less to invest in expansion, new hires, and innovation—in other words, businesses have less to spend on activities that spur economic growth.

In the second instance, government *directly competes* with private businesses by offering similar products and services to the public.

State and local governments may present the best examples of this displacement problem.

Many localities, for instance, build big public recreation centers with pools, racquetball courts, and workout facilities. That sounds great, and they're certainly fun to use, so what's the problem?

The problem is that government is competing with privately owned businesses. Backed by the power to issue bonds to finance the rec center's construction and the power to tax its citizens to pay for the annual operating expenses (things our businessperson can't do), the local government is able to eliminate much of the usual financial risk associated with a recreation center and—whether it intends to or not—is able to *eliminate competition* from the private sector.

Now, I'm not saying this is some nefarious government plot. Often good people in government genuinely want to do nice things for their citizens. What I *am* saying is that good intentions by government can often have unintended and harmful consequences, and we need to be aware of them.

Let's look at more unintended consequences of the government rec center. Even if a neighborhood needed and could support a recreation center, our private businessman and his potential investors would have to worry about the local government's swooping into the neighborhood after their private center was built simply because the government determined that the neighborhood could use another rec center. The government's decision wouldn't usually be based on responsible market studies—as the private businessman's was—but on the mere desires of bureaucrats and politicians who weren't spending their own money and didn't have to consider the risk of the project's failing.

The government rec center might even underprice our private-sector one, because, again, the government doesn't need to be as concerned about losing money on the venture. After all, it could just raise taxes when it needed to cover the losses that would inevitably occur (very few ventures run by government ever turn a profit or are even self-sustaining).

As a result of the unfair competition of the government-owned rec center, not only is the businessperson essentially prevented from doing business (his liberty—his opportunity to pursue happiness—is curtailed), but the citizens are also harmed because *everyone* has to pay for the rec center through their taxes, even if they *never use it*. In addition, the citizens may not get any competing local rec centers to move in and offer better equipment, better hours, or more customer service–oriented staff, because few businesspeople are going to build a recreation center when there's a possibility that the government could move in anytime, unfairly compete, and put it out of business.

Because government's ability to crowd out private activity not only reduces economic efficiencies and the power of the free market, but also the *opportunities* of entrepreneurs and the *choices* of consumers, citizens' liberty once again finds itself reduced to a smaller and smaller sliver of the liberty pie.

Finally, the third way in which increased government spending reduces liberty is that it requires either higher current taxes or higher future taxes to pay for that spending, and that means less money you get to keep and fewer choices you get to make about how to spend what you earn. Let's explore this in further detail under the taxation factor of liberty pie.

Taxation

WHEN POLITICIANS TALK about higher taxes, we're used to hearing about the positive or negative economic consequences such tax increases will have. But few people ever translate those impacts into the consequences for liberty.

How do higher taxes reduce your liberty? The most obvious way

241

is that every dollar government takes from you is one dollar less you can spend on food, medicine, shelter, or whatever else you might choose to spend your money on. If the government increases your taxes by $1,000 a year because it has decided it knows how to spend that $1,000 better than you do, that $1,000 annual loss reduces your choices in life immediately. It means you'll be able to buy fewer groceries for your family; you won't be able to put that money toward your child's college fund as you had planned; you'll have to save longer to get that car you needed; you'll have to forgo that advertising to grow your small business; or you'll have to work overtime to make up the difference.

But that tax increase also negatively affects us even further into the future because we lose the benefit of the compounding ability of that $1,000 over time. For example, one of the things you can't do with that $1,000 that the government takes from you every year is invest it in your *own* future economic growth—whether that's in an interest-bearing bank savings account, the stock market, or your own business. It's a reduction of your future opportunities—shrinking your liberty even more.

And let's not forget about the even longer-term effect of that money taken out of your pocket today: Because government will never spend that $1,000 more efficiently than you would have, the total amount of real economic activity in America will be reduced by that inefficiency. So that $1,000 may only equate, for example, to $800 in real economic activity after $200 was taken off the top to pay for the federal bureaucracy it was filtered through. Multiply that inefficiency by every single taxpayer, and you can see a giant drop in real economic activity in America. And all that reduced economic efficiency adds up to an enormous loss of opportunities and choices. *That's* the liberty impact.

The fact that higher taxes result in less economic activity is not new. It's not even a particularly Republican concept, as President

John F. Kennedy spoke about it, too. In a 1963 message to Congress on tax reduction and reform, he stated:

> Our tax system still siphons out of the private economy too large a share of personal and business purchasing power and reduces the incentive for risk, investment and effort—thereby aborting our recoveries and stifling our national growth rate.

Similarly, in a 1963 radio and television address to the nation on his tax reduction bill, President Kennedy stated:

> A tax cut means higher family income and higher business profits and a balanced federal budget. Every taxpayer and his family will have more money left over after taxes for a new car, a new home, new conveniences, education and investment. Every businessman can keep a higher percentage of his profits in his cash register or put it to work expanding or improving his business, and as the national income grows, the federal government will ultimately end up with more revenues.

A simple way to think of liberty in the economic sphere is to remember that *liberty in the economy means opportunity:* opportunity to buy, to save and invest, to donate to charity, to grow a business, to succeed, and, yes, even to fail.

Put in terms of the liberty pie, taxes transfer a huge portion of the citizens' liberty slice over to the government power slice. The larger and more excessive government is, the more money it requires from the citizens to sustain it, and the less freedom those citizens have to spend money on the things that they need or want.

When the government increases your taxes, it doesn't just take your hard-earned money, it also reduces your choices today and your opportunities in the future.

Big Government Has Divided Our Nation

THROUGH INCREASED REGULATIONS, taxes, and spending, we've seen how big government has harmed our economy and our liberty. But big government has also harmed our civility and unity as a nation.

One reason there's so much political angst and division today among Americans is precisely because government has grown so powerful and intrusive in our daily lives, in our economy, and in our businesses.

It should make us all nervous when we realize that the laws that govern our lives—our take-home pay, how we're allowed to raise our children, and what products we can and can't own—can be changed every two to four years depending on who's in power in Washington, in our states, or even in our towns. Depending on who's in charge, governments can tighten regulations to make finding a job harder, they can make a legal activity illegal, they can raise taxes so we can't afford a second car to get to work, and they can tell us what medicines we're allowed to take and whether we'll have to give up our homes to the next big-box store that moves into town.

We've given governments at all levels so much power that now every major election has become a battle for our very different and often incompatible philosophies of life—conservatives versus liberals versus libertarians versus moderates. As a result, political discourse often lacks civility, people are angry with candidates and their supporters, and the country becomes more divided the bigger government grows. Until we start reducing government's role, every election will become "the most important election in our lifetimes," and every election will only serve to divide us more, because every election will continue to be about whose philosophy will be running our lives for the next four years.

If government were smaller, limited to the most basic functions for which it was originally intended, it would play a much smaller role in our lives and we would have fewer things to disagree about and fewer reasons to fight.

As the founders so wisely intended, the federal government should be focused primarily on the task of defending the nation and protecting life, liberty, and order, while leaving much of the rest of governing to the states. While this means that we'd still have arguments about how big and intrusive government gets at the state level, state governments are more accessible and accountable to their citizens. And if some citizens ultimately find that they can't live under the regulations, taxes, and spending of their state governments, they at least have forty-nine other options from which to choose.

Time to Wake Up

PRESIDENT RONALD REAGAN once admonished us as a nation that

> Freedom is never more than one generation away from extinction. We didn't pass it to our children in the bloodstream. It must be fought for, protected, and handed on for them to do the same, or one day we will spend our sunset years telling our children and our children's children what it was once like in the United States where men were free.

Politicians are voting on an almost daily basis to appropriate our money, our property, and our rights, and to make us subjects rather

245

than citizens. We must be wary of those who promise to solve every problem with a new law, or to fix income inequality with a new tax, or to "create" jobs or healthier citizens with a new spending program. While efforts to solve society's problems may seem laudable, are the solutions things that government can or should do? If so, at what price to liberty? And not just to *your* liberty, which you may be willing to give up, but to the liberty of other citizens and of future generations, on whose behalf you have no right to make such irreversible decisions.

As I've said throughout this book, America faces some of the most significant and unprecedented erosions of liberty in our lifetimes. The federal government commanded us to buy private insurance or face a penalty; the EPA is attempting to regulate our lives by regulating the by-products of practically everything we buy and everything we do; the National Labor Relations Board intimidated companies to not do business in twenty-three right-to-work states; and the administration tried to appease environmentalists by ignoring the authority of Congress in an attempt to stop the mining of one of America's most abundant energy sources.

There are those who have contended that this disregard for the law is perfectly acceptable because the policy ends justify the lawless means. They've said the Constitution is outdated and not flexible enough for a government that must grow to meet the needs of a growing nation. They've argued that the Founding Fathers couldn't have possibly predicted the America of today and all the issues we face, such as the uninsured, the mortgage crisis, and our environmental debates.

But the Founding Fathers knew that no matter what age in history—whether 1776 or 2013—leaders not bound by a set of laws would always seek power and control at the cost of their fellow citizens' liberty.

That's why no matter which political party is in control in Washington, it will always be necessary for the states and the people to serve as watchdogs over their government. Sadly, the attempt to steal liberty by Congress, by a president, or by the courts will happen again. If history shows us anything, it's that over time, governments seek to centralize and accumulate power. And governments don't accumulate power to *not* use it. That's why we must remain vigilant.

We also can no longer be silent or shy about speaking up for a philosophy of limited government that promotes liberty, prosperity, and human flourishing over a philosophy that's been shown time and again to eventually lead to despotism and shared suffering. It's incumbent upon all of us to communicate to our friends and families how America's first principles relate to today's government policies, such as taxation, transportation, welfare, jobs, regulation, mandates on religious institutions, and managing the economy. Simple illustrations such as the liberty pie help us to do that, and they work.

I know this because I've run four times for public office as an outspoken, unapologetic limited-government conservative talking about constitutional, conservative principles. Each time my opponents significantly outspent me, and yet, each time I won. Three of those wins were in one of the bluest parts of northern Virginia, and the fourth win was with the largest number of votes any candidate for attorney general had ever received in Virginia history.

I won not just because I had lots of committed supporters who worked hard for me, but because I didn't compromise on first principles. Instead I *explained* them. I explained to voters how those principles were critical to preserving life, liberty, and the opportunity to pursue happiness for *all* citizens. I explained how liberty coupled with personal responsibility provides economic opportunity and the chance for prosperity, allows us the choice of what careers to pursue, gives us the freedom to buy products and services that make life easier or just make us happier, and allows us the ability to freely speak our minds and practice the religions of our choice.

But I even have an example more recent than my four elections.

In the 2012 presidential election in Virginia, Barack Obama won with 51 percent of the vote. Yet, a ballot initiative (one I'm proud to say I helped write) on a very conservative principle—defending property rights against state and local government eminent domain abuse—won with an astounding 74 percent of the vote. That property rights constitutional amendment passed despite the fact that the Democrat Party handed out sample ballots across the state urging people to vote against it, claiming it would cost government more money and bring economic development to a halt.

The conclusion I've drawn from my own experiences is that constitutionally based conservative principles—when explained properly—win. People start listening when it's explained to them that a government powerful enough to give them everything they want is also a government powerful enough to take away everything they have.

That Democrat coal miner in Southwest Virginia certainly started listening when he lost his job because the administration began abusing its power to shut down the coal mines. That independent-voting aircraft mechanic who didn't want to be forced to join a union just to get a decent job started listening, too. And that once-politically ambivalent family that could barely pay their mortgage started listening when they also struggled to pay their electric bills, which went up because of new EPA regulations.

The battles I've described in this book aren't about being opponents of government or of a political party; they are about being *proponents of liberty.*

This effort isn't about one presidential or midterm election. This is about a movement. This is about spreading the message of liberty and limited government.

The long-term battle is to change the hearts and minds of our fellow Americans, so they come to understand that allowing the government to grow a little more powerful to achieve something they want today will inevitably result in government's using that same power to take away more of their liberty tomorrow. It's a gradual process to wake the American people up after they've been conditioned for five generations that bigger government is better government.

But this is a battle we can win. More importantly, this is a battle we *must* win.

Our Founding Fathers pledged their lives, their fortunes, and their sacred honor to break from tyranny and create a nation where people would be forever free. More than a million people have given their lives throughout our history to defend that gift of liberty and pass it on to succeeding generations.

Today, continuing the fight to preserve that gift against an ever-encroaching government doesn't involve sacrificing our lives or our fortunes. For us, it's as simple as getting off the couch, talking to our friends and families about founding principles, holding public officials to those principles, supporting candidates who will support the Constitution, and voting. There's no physical danger for anyone who does that. And there's too much at stake to stay home and be idle. For, as Ronald Reagan said, if we lose freedom here, there's no place to escape to. This is the last stand on earth.

We owe no less than our fullest effort to ourselves, our predecessors, and our posterity to cherish that precious gift of liberty, to defend it, and to recruit others to its cause so that we can live in a nation where our elected leaders return to our founding vision, where liberty and personal responsibility once again trump political expediency, and where the people reclaim their rightful sovereignty—a nation where this great American experiment does not find its conclusion, but instead forever remains a beacon of freedom, opportunity, and hope for the world.

ACKNOWLEDGMENTS

MY BIGGEST DEBT of gratitude is to my wife, Teiro, for her sacrifices and support, not just while I was working on this book, but in all aspects of my life. She is my inspiration and my motivation. I also want to thank my children—Alie, Marielle, Reilly, Reagan, Annie, Jack, and Max—for sacrificing their time with their dad and for their constant love (and in the case of the boys, their constant pounding . . .).

There are several folks with whom I have worked to actively carry out the federalism fights I catalogue in this book. Their intellectual firepower and legal abilities have allowed Virginia to have the successes we have had. These folks include Virginia Solicitor General Duncan Getchell; law school classmate and Deputy Attorney General Wes Russell; and former Senior Appellate Counsel Steve McCullough (who had the temerity to leave the attorney general's office to be appointed a Virginia appellate judge). Wes and Duncan were also extremely generous in their willingness to read drafts of the book and offer many insightful comments that have resulted in a better final product.

Our legal team has included participation and support from many talented people in the Virginia Office of the Attorney General, including, but not limited to, Deputy Attorneys General Rick Neel, David Johnson, Mike Favale, John Childrey, and Rita Beale; Amanda McGuire, Mike Brady, Kimberly Taylor, Elizabeth Andrews, and Jeff Allen. And these legal efforts have been ably herded (like cats) first by the then Chief Deputy Attorney General Chuck James and, more recently, by Chief Deputy Attorney General Trish West.

Many others have played supporting roles in making the efforts you read about in this book possible. They include LaToya Gray, Juliana Comer, Jan Myer, Caroline Gibson, Sara Kennedy, Katie Courain, Noah Rogers, Cory Chenard, Dan Dodds, Ryan Sneddon, Lt. Jeff Weinmeister, Sharon Mangrum, and Harrison Clark.

Noah and Meredith Wall have played unique supporting roles that contributed to the final effort in this book, particularly in their sometimes-desperate attempts to keep me from shooting myself in the foot.

I would also be remiss if I didn't mention my fellow Republican attorneys general who have taken up so many federalism fights themselves. Our partnership to man the last line of defense has been something I've been honored to be a part of, and their tenacity always gives me renewed optimism for America. They include Luther Strange of Alabama, Tom Horne of Arizona, John Suthers of Colorado, Pam Bondi, and her predecessor Bill McCollum, of Florida, Sam Olens of Georgia, Alan Wilson of South Carolina, my neighbor Patrick Morrisey of West Virginia, Bill Schuette, and his predecessor Mike Cox, of Michigan, Greg Zoeller of Indiana, Mark Shurtleff of Utah, Wayne Stenehjem of North Dakota, Marty Jackley of South Dakota, Jon Bruning of Nebraska, Derek Schmidt of Kansas, Greg Abbott of Texas, Mike DeWine of Ohio, J. B. Van Hollen of Wisconsin, Lawrence Wasden of Idaho, Buddy Caldwell of Louisiana, Rob McKenna of Washington, and Scott Pruitt of Oklahoma.

The Virginia Tea Party Patriot Federation made the passage of Virginia's Health Care Freedom Act its legislative priority in 2010, and the combined efforts of so many local Tea Party groups were singularly effective in the passage of that legislation that ultimately served as the basis of Virginia's Obamacare lawsuit. I truly appreciate their commitment to first principles.

Over the course of writing this book, I spent many nights as the beneficiary of Jackie Gottstein's patience and hospitality while I worked with Brian to write, edit, and revise this book. And true to her Italian heritage, she fed me well, and is just a complete pleasure to spend time with. I also appreciate her patience in allowing Brian so much dedicated time to work on this book, as he is already kept pretty busy with the outrageous demands of his boss at work . . .

Which brings me to Brian Gottstein. For all his gruffness, at heart he is a softie, and it's been a pleasure to go through the effort of putting this book together with him. It's been a new experience for both of us, but he brought an organized professionalism to our efforts that made us much more efficient, and his dedication was the single-most critical factor to us producing something that I think we are both happy with. I appreciate Brian's shared appreciation for the history and principles represented in the subject matter of this book and his doggedness in pushing us through our workload to complete this project. I can't imagine going through this effort with someone who was not a friend. Fortunately, I didn't have to worry about that.

Index

About the Author

KEN CUCCINELLI became attorney general of Virginia in 2010 and serves as the attorney for the government of the commonwealth and its agencies, providing them with legal advice and representing them in legal matters.

Besides the typical duties of representing the commonwealth, prosecuting sexual predators and those who commit fraud, and protecting the elderly and the incapacitated from abuse and neglect, he has been a leader in the fight against the unconstitutional overreach of the federal government.

He has also been a champion for property rights, helping to write and advocate for a state constitutional amendment to dramatically curb the state's eminent domain power, so government can no longer take land from one private owner and give it to another merely for the purpose of increasing tax revenues, economic development, or private gain.

Prior to serving as attorney general, he served in the Senate of Virginia from 2002 to 2010. As a state senator and private attorney, he worked to improve the commonwealth's mental health system, getting legislation passed that provided for more humane treatment of the mentally ill.

As a senator, he also worked to make government more transparent and accountable to its citizens by fighting for a law to put the state's detailed budget online in a format that citizens could easily understand.

Known throughout his political career for holding both Republicans and Democrats to the principles of limited government, his fidelity to our founding principles and to the Constitution comes before party or politics.

Mr. Cuccinelli earned a degree in mechanical engineering from the University of Virginia, a master's degree in international commerce and policy from George Mason University, and his juris doctor from the George Mason University School of Law and Economics.

He is running for governor of Virginia in 2013.

3/30